LEARNING ALL THE TIME

JOHN HOLT

LEARNING ALL THE TIME

Education Now Publishing Cooperative Limited
Lighthouse Books

First published in 1989 in the United States of America by Addison-Wesley Publishing Company, Inc., Reading, Massachusetts.

First published in Great Britain in 1991 by Education Now Publishing Co-operative Ltd., P.O.Box 186, Ticknall, Derbyshire, DE7 1WF, in association with Lighthouse Books, 55 Mint Road, Liss, Hants. GU33 7DQ.

Reprinted 1991

Copyright © 1989 by Holt Associates Reprinted 1991

British Libary Cataloguing in Publication Data
Holt, John, *1923 -*
    Learning all the time.
    1. Learning
    I. Title
    155.413   155. 413 HOL

    ISBN 1-871526-04-3

Acknowledgements

Grateful acknowledgement is made to Harvard University Press for permission to reprint portions of *Gnys at Wrk* by Glenda Bissex, copyright (C) 1980 by the President and Fellows of Harvard College.

Portions of Chapter 1 appeared earlier in *The New Boston Review* and *The Atlantic Monthly*, and portions of Chapter 6 in *The Progressive*.

Many of the designations used by manufacturers and sellers to distinguish their products are claimed as trademarks. Where those designations appear in this book and the publishers were aware of a copyright claim, the designations have been printed in initial capital letters (e.g. Lego, M&M's).

In accordance with legal requirements the publishers make the following affirmation: ' The moral right of the author has been asserted'.

Printed in Great Britain by BPCC Wheatons Ltd, Essex.

BOOKS BY JOHN HOLT

How Children Fail
How Children Learn
The Underachieving School
What Do I Do Monday?
Freedom and Beyond
Escape from Childhood
Instead of Education
Never Too Late
Teach Your Own
Learning All the Time

JOHN HOLT

The most striking thing about John's writing is its firm, straightforward good sense. He never derives theory from theory, but stays as close as possible to experience itself. His entire career was really based on this, this *making sense of experience*. One of the finest things about him was the underlying motive of all that thought: he truly wanted to make the world a better place for mankind. And it was the world he was thinking of at all times, not just the field of education—as if that could be isolated from everything else. This overarching care antedated his own career as a teacher. It was a lifelong care and he labored in behalf of it with remarkable patience, tenacity, forbearance, and generosity. He was one of the few people I have ever known who could condemn the sin and forgive the sinner. In the heat of argument he never became unkind and never abandoned his own great loyalty to reason. If one wanted to know the meaning of ethics one had only to look at John Holt's ordinary courtesies. This is a way of saying, too, that he was an authentically civilized man—a rare, rare creature. His procedure as a writer was an extension of his character. The appeal to reason and to experience is in fact the most civilized of procedures. It chastens the ego and defers correctly to things that are truly great. It is modest and at the same time confident and even adventurous.

George Dennison
October 1985

C O N T E N T S

EDITOR'S FOREWORD

Early in 1982, John Holt began to write a book about how children learn to read and write and count at home—with very little or no teaching. Around the same time, while listening wryly to expansive promises from politicians to pour more money into the schools and extend greater federal authority and control over education, he had (only half-jokingly) proposed another book, to be called "How to Make Schools Worse." Being by nature optimistic and constructive, however, he had given up the notion of a polemic and focused more and more on the very nature of early learning, as it takes place in the everyday lives of small children. By the spring of 1983 he put into words exactly what this new book would be about:

> The book will be a *demonstration* [italics his] that children, without being coerced or manipulated, or being put in exotic, specially prepared environments, or having their thinking planned and ordered for them, can, will, and do pick up from the world around them important information about what we call the Basics.
>
> It will also demonstrate that "ordinary" people, without special training and often without large amounts of schooling themselves, can give their children whatever slight assistance may be needed to help them in their exploration of the world, and that to do this task requires no more than a little tact, patience, attention, and readily available information.

He continued for the next two years writing parts of the book, many of which appeared in the magazine he edited, and which his colleagues at Holt Associates still publish: *Growing without Schooling*. Lectures that he gave during this time often developed the theme of "natural learning" or "the three R's at home." The many small children who played and worked in the Holt Associates office constantly stimulated and refined his insights.

In June of 1984, concerned that his publishers, or future readers, might misconstrue his purpose, he wrote us a long letter distinguishing his book from the many others flooding the bookstores on "early" learning:

This is not a book about "How to Help Your Child Succeed in School." It is a book about children learning. By learning I mean making more sense of the world around them. (let me try this again) Learning, to me, means making more sense of the world around us, and being able to do more things in it. Success in school means remembering the answers to teachers' questions, getting clever about guessing what questions they will ask, and about how to fool them when you don't know the answers. Years ago, even before my first book came out, I was for a while tutoring an eighth-grader, who was having some troubles in school. One day she asked me, with great seriousness, "How *do* you learn about history?" Taking her question as seriously as she meant it, I said, "I think you may be asking me two questions: one, how do I learn more about history, and two, how do I get better grades in history class in school? The first thing to understand is that these are completely different and separate activities, having almost nothing to do with each other. If you want to learn more about how to find out about what things were like in the past, I can give you some hints about that. And if you want to find out how to get better grades in your History class, I can give you some hints about that. But they will not be the same hints." She understood and accepted this, and asked me for both kinds of hints, which I gave her. In this book I will for the most part be discussing the first of these two questions—what sorts of things might we do to make various aspects of the world more accessible, interesting, and transparent to children.

John Holt died in September of 1985, before he could finish this book. Since he had outlined so clearly what the book was to cover and had written so much of it, in draft, in the magazine, in letters, or elsewhere, it was possible to assemble the book according to his design. In a few instances, when articles he had written earlier spoke directly to the themes he had laid out, these have been woven in with appropriate chapters and identified with a footnote.

The publishers wish to thank Nancy Wallace and Susannah Sheffer for much thoughtful editorial assistance. We are also grateful to Pat Farenga, Donna Richoux, and all the staff of Holt Associates for considerable help in making this publication possible. Each of these close colleagues and friends of John Holt's is involved in furthering his ideas and beliefs and helped us shoulder the difficult responsibility of editing and publishing a posthumous book.

The wealth of material called for painful choices, anticipated by John himself: "We are probably going to find ourselves with much more material than we will have room for ... cutting and squeezing, not puffing up, is going to be the task." He went on to say, "I think we have something pretty good here, and am eager to get ahead with it."

M.L. 6/14/89

Learning All the Time

Reading and Writing

The world of books was first
opened to Anna, she came to be a
citizen of it, when for the first
time she clutched a book in her
hand and thought, "This book is
mine."

Reading and Trust

Once I visited a family whose youngest child, then about five, I had not seen in several years. After sizing me up for a while from a distance, and deciding that I seemed to be OK, she made friends, and soon asked me if I would "help her read." Not quite knowing what she meant, I said I would. She got her book, Dr. Seuss's *Hop on Pop*, led me to a sofa, and, when I was seated, climbed up, snuggled against me, and began slowly to read out loud. Apparently the first thing she had to do, before the work could begin, was to get in cozy physical contact with me.

In *The Lives of Children*, describing his work with twelve-year-old José, the tough street kid, George Dennison makes the same point. He could work with José only when the two of them were alone in a locked room. Of these meetings Dennison writes:

> And so our base of operations was our own relationship; and since José early came to trust me, I was able to do something which, simple as it may sound, was of the utmost importance: I made the real, the deeper base of our relationship a matter of physical contact. I could put my arm around his shoulders, or hold his arm, or sit close to him so that our bodies touched.... The importance of this contact to a child experiencing problems with reading can hardly be overestimated.

I have to add here that the trusting had to come *before* the touching. To touch or hold a child who has not yet decided to trust you will only make that child far more nervous.

In any case, whether you are a "gifted" five-year-old or a terrified, illiterate twelve-year-old, trying to read something new is a dangerous adventure. You may make mistakes, or fail, and so feel disappointment or shame, or anger, or disgust. Just in order to get started on this adventure, most people need as much comfort, reassurance, and security as they can find. The typical classroom, with other children ready to point out, correct, and even laugh at every mistake, and the teacher all too often (wittingly or unwittingly) helping and urging them to do this, is the worst possible place for a child to begin.

At the Ny Lille Skole (New Little School), near Copenhagen, which I described in *Instead of Education*, there is no formal reading program at all—no classes, no reading groups, no instruction, no testing, nothing. Children (like adults) read if, and when, and what, and with whom, and as much as they want to. But all the children know—it is not announced, just one of those things you find out by being in the school—that anytime they want, they can go to Rasmus Hansen, a tall, deep-voiced, slow-speaking teacher (for many years the head teacher of the school), and say, "Will you read with me?" and he will say, "Yes." The child picks something to read, goes with Rasmus to a little nook, not a locked room but a cozy and private place, sits down right beside him, and begins to read aloud. Rasmus does almost nothing. From time to time he says softly, *"Ja, Ja,"* implying "That's right, keep going." Unless he suspects the child may be getting into a panic, he almost never points out or corrects a mistake. If asked for a word, he simply says what it is. After a while, usually about twenty minutes or so, the child stops, closes the book, gets up, and goes off to do something else.

One could hardly call this teaching. Yet, as it happens, Rasmus was trained as a reading teacher. He told me that it had taken him many years to stop doing—one at a time—all the many things he had been trained to do, and finally to learn that this tiny amount of moral support and help was all that children needed of him, and that anything more was of no help at all.

Thirty Hours

I asked Rasmus how much of this "help" children seemed to need before they felt ready to explore reading on their own. He said that from his records of these reading sessions he had found that the longest amount of time any of the children spent reading with him was about thirty hours, usually in sessions of twenty minutes to a half hour, spread out over a few months. But, he added, many children spent much less time than that with him, and many others never read with him at all. I should add that almost all of the children went from the Ny Lille Skole to the gymnasium, a high school far more difficult and demanding than all but a few secondary schools in the U.S. However and whenever the children may have learned it, they were all good readers.

Thirty hours. I had met that figure before. Years earlier, I had served for a few weeks as a consultant to a reading program for adult illiterates in Cleveland, Ohio. Most of the students were from thirty to fifty years old; most were poor; about half were black, half white; most had moved to Cleveland either from Appalachia or the deep South. There were three sessions, each lasting three weeks. In each session, students went to classes for two hours a night, five nights a week: that is, thirty hours. To teach them, the teachers used Caleb Gattegno's *Words in Color*, a very ingenious (I now think, too ingenious) method. Used well, it can be very effective. But it makes great demands on teachers. That is, it can be used very badly. Few of the volunteer teachers in the program had previously used *Words in Color*; they themselves had been trained in an intensive course just before they began to teach the illiterates. I observed a good many of the teachers in one of the three sessions. Most of them used the method fairly well, one or two very well, a few very badly. The students and classes themselves varied; some classes were much more supportive, some students much more bold and vigorous than others. I don't know what, if any, follow-up studies of the program were ever made, or what the students did with their newfound skill. My strong impression at the end of my three weeks was that most of the students in the classes I had observed had learned enough about reading in their thirty hours so that they could go on exploring and reading, and could become as skillful *as they wanted to be*, on their own.

Some years later I first heard of Paulo Freire, a Brazilian educator and reformer, who, until the army ran him out of the country, had been teaching reading and writing to illiterate adult peasants in the very poorest villages. One might say that his method was a kind of politically radical, grown-up version of the method Sylvia Ashton-Warner described in her books *Spinster* and *Teacher*. That is, he began by talking with these peasants about the conditions and problems of their lives (this was what the army didn't like), and then showed them how to write and read the words that came up most in their talk. He too found that it took only about thirty hours of teaching before these wretchedly poor and previously demoralized peasants were able to go on exploring reading on their own.

Thirty hours. One school week. That is the true size of the task.

Discovering Letters

O nce again, a child has reminded me how various, ingenious, and unexpected are children's ways of exploring the world around them, in particular the world of letters and numbers. My teacher in this case was five-year-old Chris, a happy and energetic boy who comes to my office almost every day with his mother, Mary, and is now completely at home here.

His father drives a very large tow truck, the kind that is used for towing other trucks, so it is not surprising that many of Chris's favorite toys are little cars and trucks, some of them tow trucks. He has a kind of track for these trucks to run on, a collection of straight, curved, and other pieces, which he joins together to make a highway, complete with overpasses, intersections, and so on. One of his favorite games, which he plays for hours, is running his cars and trucks around this roadway in various complicated ways, all the while making up some story to go with them, mixed now and then with the wavering note of a police car. A couple of times in the past months he has noticed that some of the pieces of this roadway, by themselves or joined with another piece or two, make a shape that looks like a letter, and once in a while he will show me one of these shapes and perhaps tell, perhaps ask, me what it is. But he has not done this very often; he is mostly interested in the trucks as trucks and the road as a road.

6

Today, while lying on the floor playing with the trucks, he pointed out to me as I walked by that one of his pieces of road made the leter *J*, another the letter *T*, and another (with a little use of the imagination) the letter *I*. He had several *J*-pieces, and began putting some of his "letters" together and asking me what the words said. I pronounced them as best I could, easy when there was a vowel in the word, hard when there wasn't, in which case I would make some kind of hissing and sputtering noise.

A little later, walking by him, I pointed out that a big section of his road had made a very large letter *U*, so once again he began making "words" and asking me what they said. After a number of imaginary and/or unpronounceable words, I put the *J* on one side of the big *U* and the *T* on the other, and said they made a real word, *jut*. He took note of that, without showing any great interest. A little later he found a piece that would work as a letter *S*, so after pronouncing a number of other nonwords and seeing the letters *J*, *T*, *I*, and *S* close to the big *U*, I made the word *jitsu* from *jujitsu*, which he knew. Again, he noted the fact, but did not ask me for any other real words, nor did I press the matter.

He continued with this a short while longer, and then stopped, turning to one of the hundred or more other projects he invents to pass and enjoy the time. Not long after, his mother and Steve, who also works in the office, began to assemble a large number of packages of books, to load on a hand truck to take to the post office, and soon Chris rushed to help. Any time a job comes up that involves moving large objects, he wants to be part of it. Like many little children, he loves struggling with packages or other objects that he can just barely lift and hold; it makes him feel stronger, more capable, more useful, and closer to the world of grown-ups.

From time to time, in sudden bursts, Chris returned

to his letter games. What has he learned from these games, beyond the names and shapes of the letters he now knows? Among other things, that letters are made-up shapes; that not all shapes are letters; that letters can be joined together to make words; that not all combinations of letters make words that sound good or mean anything; that shapes or objects designed to be seen or used one way can be seen or used in other very different ways; and that doing this is often interesting and exciting. All this knowledge of shapes and numbers he has made for himself out of his own experience, for his own reasons. He really knows it and will never forget it. It is as much a part of him as his arms and legs. He has not learned it to please me, though it may please him, now and then, to show me that he knows it. With great but patient curiosity, I wait for the next time he may choose to show me something else he has learned, in this busy office where he is free to explore.

Exploring Words

L*et's Read* is the title of a book by Leonard Bloomfield and Clarence Barnhart, which could help many children *teach themselves* to read. This was not the authors' idea—they meant parents to use the book to teach their children to read. I think doing this is not useful or necessary and will in most cases be harmful. Learning to read is easy, and most children will do it more quickly and better and with more pleasure if they can do it themselves, untaught, untested, and helped only when and if they ask for help.

This book and others like it, however, can be useful for children. After sixty-odd pages of unnecessary instructions comes the good and helpful part of the book. At the top of the page are all the one-syllable English words that end in -an: can, Dan, fan, man, Nan, pan, ran, tan, an, ban, van. Then come a number of short sentences using these words. Next come the -at words—bat, cat, fat, hat, mat, Nat, pat, rat, sat, at, tat, vat—with sentences using both -an and -at words. The next page has -ad words, and the next pages, in order, words ending in -ap, -ag, -am, -ab, -al, then -ig, -in, -id, and so on. We could of course figure out those words for ourselves, but it is handy to have them all printed out, in big print. Each page has sentences using the new words of that page, plus all the words that went before. They don't make very interesting stories, but, as the authors rightly point out, at this stage children find it exciting enough just to figure out what the words say. Later, when they have more words to work with, the stories get a little better. But by the time children work their way to page 100 (or even much sooner), they will know enough about how the reading game works to start puzzling out real books, magazines, signs, cereal boxes, and so on.

A book like this is best for a child to browse through. When my niece was about four, I gave the book to my sister, thinking she might use it to teach her daughter. However, neither my niece nor, later, her younger brother would stand for being taught—they just refused to go along. But the book was left in sight where the little girl could get at it, and she was encouraged to think of it as hers. Certain pages are covered with little brown marks that I take to be her fingerprints. She must have spent quite a few months looking at those pages, thinking about them, before she figured out the system and went on to look at other books. I wasn't there when she was teaching herself to read, and as she did most of the work in private, often with her door shut, asking very few questions of anyone, no one knows exactly what she did.

I would guess that many little children would like to browse through such a book. It is big, grown-up, and official looking, obviously not a "children's" book. There are only four pages of line drawings in it; all else is print. But much of the print is large enough to be easy for little children to see, and many of the words are small enough to be easy for them to figure out. If I had young children, I would give them this book (along with others), and let them decide how they wanted to use it—if at all. If a child asked me to read it aloud, I would, perhaps moving my finger under the words as I read them. Though, on second thought, I suspect that some children would take this to be teaching and make me stop doing it. If the child asked questions about this word or that, I would answer. Otherwise, I would leave the child and the book alone.

Reading Readiness

Our professional experts on the teaching of reading have advocated a great many foolish things, but none more foolish than the notion that the way to get children "ready to read" is to show them a lot of books full of nothing but pictures and ask them a lot of silly questions about them.

The proper analogy can be found, as is so often true, with children learning to speak, that extraordinary intellectual feat we all accomplished before the adults got it into their heads that they could "teach" us. Children get ready to speak by hearing speech all around them. The important thing about that speech is that the adults, for the most part, are *not* talking in order to give children a model. They are talking to each other because they have things to say. So the first thing the baby intuits, figures out, about the speech of adults, is that it is *serious*. Adults talk to make things happen. They talk, and things *do* happen. The baby thinks, feels, that this is a pretty serious activity, well worth doing.

When I was a kid, I taught myself to read, as many children do. Nobody taught me, and, as far as I can remember, nobody helped me very much or read aloud to me. When we were a little older, a grandmother read aloud to my sister and me, but by then we were already skillful readers. She read the Dr. Doolittle books by Hugh Lofting, and to sit on the sofa, one on each side, was a very happy scene, all the more so because she read these stories with the greatest seriousness, without a touch of sentimentality or condescension, no "cute" inflections in her voice.

One of the things that made me want to read was that in those days (long, long ago) children's books had very few pictures in them. The few they contained were magnificent, many painted by Andrew Wyeth's father, N. C. Wyeth. Pirates, knights, Scottish Highland chiefs— great pictures. But there weren't enough of them in any one book to give me any idea of what the stories were about, so I realized that to find out what those pictures meant I was going to have to read the book. Which I soon learned to do.

What children need to get ready for reading is exposure to a lot of *print*. Not pictures, but print. They need to bathe their eyes in print, as when smaller they bathe their ears in talk. After a while, as they look at more and more print, these meaningless forms, curves, and squiggles begin to steady down, take shape, become recognizable, so that the children, without yet knowing what letters or words are, begin to see, as I once did myself, after looking at a page of print in an Indian typeface, that *this* letter appears *here*, and that group of letters appears *there*, and again *there*. When they've learned to *see* the letters and words, they are ready to ask themselves questions about what they mean and what they say. But not before—just as, when I am learning a foreign language, there is no use telling me that such and such word means such and such a thing until my ears have become sharp enough to pick it out from other people's talk.

All of which leads to a concrete suggestion. I propose that anyone who wants to make it easier for children to *discover* how to read should use as one of the "reading readiness materials" the large-print edition of the *New York Times*. The print is large enough for children to see and recognize. The paper is clearly a part of the adult world, and therefore attractive. It is serious. It has real information in it. It can be put on walls, but is not so precious that one has to worry about its being torn or defaced.

Beyond this, I would suggest that we put into the visual environment of young children, both in school and out, and not just in the prereading years but for a while thereafter, all kinds of written stuff from the adult world. Thus, among other things, timetables, road maps, ticket stubs, copies of letters, political posters, bills, various kinds of official forms, copies of bank statements, copies of instruction manuals from various machines, copies of contracts, warranties, and all those little throwaways that we find in banks. In short, lots of stuff from that adult world out there where all those people are doing all those mysterious and interesting things. Oh, and old telephone books, above all, classified-ad telephone books. Talk about social studies; a look at the Yellow Pages tells us more than any textbook about what people do, and what there is *to* do.

Inventing the Wheel

G*nys at Wrk*, by Glenda Bissex, is a delightful and revealing book, the detailed and loving account of how the author's son, Paul, did what Seymour Papert talked about in *Mindstorms*: that is, learned without being taught. He built for himself his own, at first crude, models of written English, and constantly refined them until they finally matched the written English of the world around him. *Gnys at Wrk* is also a splendid account and example of the ways in which sympathetic and trusting teachers can be of use to learners, not by deciding what they are to learn but by encouraging and helping them to learn what they are already busy learning. Like *Mindstorms*, it gives powerful ammunition to parents who are trying to deal with school systems and/ or to teachers and others who are trying to change them.

Paul Bissex began his writing at age five with an indignant note to his mother, who, busy talking with friends, had not noticed that the child was trying to ask her something. After trying a few times to get her attention he went away, but soon returned with this message printed on a piece of paper: RUDF. Luckily for him, his mother was perceptive enough to decode the note ("Are you deaf?"), understand its importance, and quickly give the boy the attention he had been asking for.

As the boy began to explore written English, his mother paid steady attention to the ways in which he was doing it. In her preface, Mrs. Bissex writes:

When I began taking notes about my infant son's development, I did not know I was gathering "data" for "research"; I was a mother with a propensity for writing

13

things down.... When Paul started spelling, I was amazed and fascinated. Only somewhat later did I learn of Charles Read's research on children's invented spelling. Excited by his work, I started seeing my notes as "data."...

What I hope this study offers, rather than generalizations to be "applied" to other children, is encouragement to look at individuals in the act of learning. And I do mean *act*, with all that implies of drama and action....

... A case study this detailed and extended over time would have been unmanageable were I not a parent.

In the preface, Mrs. Bissex describes how Paul felt about her research:

At the beginning, Paul was an unconscious subject, unaware of the significance of my tape recorder and notebook. When he first became aware, at about age six, he was pleased by my interest and attention. By seven, he had become an observer of his own progress. When I ... had Paul's early writings spread out on my desk, he loved to look at them with me and try to read them.... Paul had observed me writing down a question he had asked about spelling, and I inquired how he felt about my writing it down. "Then I know that when I'm older I can see the stuff I asked when I was little," he commented.

At eight he was self-conscious enough to object to obvious observation and note taking, which I then stopped.... [He] still brought his writings ... to me, sharing my sense of their importance. At nine he became a participant in the research, interested in thinking about *why* he had written or read things as he once had....

The study has become a special bond between us, an interest we share in each other's work, a mutual enjoyment of Paul's early childhood and of his growing up. I have come to appreciate certain qualities in my son that

I might not have seen except through the eyes of this study.

When I was teaching fifth grade with Bill Hull and beginning to watch and listen carefully to what children said and did in the class, I used to write down notes, in handwriting so tiny that they couldn't easily read it. They knew I was writing about them, and at first said, a little suspiciously, "What are you writing?" But as time went on and they began to understand that I did not see them as strange laboratory animals, but liked and respected them and was trying to see how the world of school looked through their eyes, they felt better about my note taking—though it would probably have been better if I had told them more specifically what I was trying to learn from their work. In other words, I could have made them more conscious partners in my research.

Many more children—I have no idea how many— seem to go from writing to reading than the other way around. *Gnys at Wrk* is by no means the first work I have read about children's invented spellings. Many years ago I read a most interesting article on the same subject by Carol Chomsky, who has done much good work in this area. One thing about her article I remember vividly. She reported that many children spelled words beginning in *tr—tree*, *train*, and so on—either with a *ch* or an *h* at the beginning. For a second this baffled me. But by this time I had learned to look for reason in children's "mistakes." I began to say "tree, train," et cetera, listening carefully to what sounds I was making, and found to my astonishment that what I was actually saying sounded very much like "chree" and "chrain."

It is worth noting that neither Glenda Bissex nor the parents of many other children who learned to write English in their own invented spelling had taught them

"phonics," or taught them to write, or even much encouraged them to write (except perhaps by their own
example). The children had been told and helped to
learn the names of the letters. From these they had
figured out for themselves which consonants made
which sounds. Like Paul Bissex, they began by leaving
vowels out of their words altogether, producing a writing much like the Speedwriting that many adults later
struggle and pay to learn.

As Mrs. Bissex makes clear in example after example,
Paul did not "learn to write," learn what schools would
call the skills of writing, so that later he could use them
to write something. From the beginning he wrote because he had something he wanted to say, often to
himself, sometimes to others:

> Paul, like his parents, wrote (and read and talked) be-
> cause what he was writing (or reading or saying) had
> meaning to him as an individual and as a cultural being.
> We humans are meaning-making creatures, and lan-
> guage—spoken and written—is an important means for
> making and sharing meanings.

In her work with Paul, Mrs. Bissex asked him many
questions about his learning, and gave him many of what
in another context might be called tests. But the purpose of these tests was not, as with almost all school
tests, to find out what he *didn't* know, or to prove that
he hadn't learned what he was supposed to have
learned. His mother knew he was learning. What she
wanted to know, and what he knew she wanted to know,
was *how* he was doing it. She was interested in his work
in the way a scientist (which she was) might be interested in the work of another scientist (which he was).
In this very important sense they were equals. She might
know more about English, but he knew more than she
did about what he knew about English and how he was

learning more, and his knowledge was at least as important to her as hers was to him.

> In setting his own tasks, Paul was able to keep them at the challenge level. He was not content to repeat his accomplishments but spontaneously moved on to harder tasks.... He set up a progression of increasingly difficult tasks for himself as many other children spontaneously do.

This is what all children do as they grow up—until they get to school. What all too often happens there is that children, seeing school challenges as threats, which they often are—if you fail to accomplish them, you stand a good risk of being shamed or even physically beaten—fall more and more *out* of the habit of challenging themselves, even outside of school: "... Inventive spellers start from the assumption that they can figure things out for themselves. Perhaps this is why so many of them learn to read before formal instruction."

This is my objection to books about "Teach Your Baby This" and "Teach Your Baby That." They are very likely to destroy children's belief that they can find things out for themselves, and to make them think instead that they can only find things out from others.

> As Kenneth Goodman ..., Charles Read ..., and Piaget [have shown], children's errors are not accidental but reflect their systems of knowledge. If teachers can regard errors as sources of information for instruction rather than mistakes to be condemned and stamped out, students ... should be able to assume this more constructive view, too.

This is exactly the point that Seymour Papert makes in *Mindstorms*. When children working with computers make "mistakes"—that is, get from their computer a result other than the one they wanted—they tend to say, if they are newly arrived from school, "It's all wrong," and they want to start over from the beginning. Papert encourages them to see that it's not *all* wrong, there's just one particular thing wrong. In computer lingo, there is a "bug" in their program and their task is to "de-bug" it—find the one false step, take it out, and replace it with the correct step.

When I taught fifth grade many of my students, filling out forms, would identify themselves as "grils." I was always touched and amused by this mistake, but I thought it was just foolish or careless. Not for many, many years did I understand that the children calling themselves "grils" were thinking sensibly, were indeed doing exactly what their teachers had told them to do— sounding out the word and spelling it a sound at a time. They had been taught, and learned, that the letters *gr* made the sound "gurr." So they wrote down *gr*. That left the sound "ul." They knew that *l* had to come at the end, and they knew that there was an *i* in the word, so obviously it had to be *gril*. Countless adults had no doubt told them that *gril* was wrong, and I joined the crowd. But it was futile; they went on trying to spell *girl* phonetically, as they had been told to, and could only come up with *gril*. If I had had the sense to say, "You folks are on the right track, only in this case English uses the letters *g-i-r* to make the sound 'gurr,'" they would have said, "Oh, I see," and could have done it correctly.

Words in Context

Children reading for their own pleasure rarely stop to ask about words. They want to get on with the story. If the word is important, they can usually make a good guess about what it is. "He drew an arrow from his quiver." Easy to see that a quiver is some sort of gadget to put arrows in. More complicated words they figure out by meeting them in many different contexts.

People learn to read well, and get big vocabularies, from *books*, not workbooks and dictionaries. As a kid I read years ahead of my age, but I never looked up words in dictionaries, and didn't even *have* a dictionary. In my lifetime I don't believe I have looked up even as many as fifty words—neither have most good readers.

Most people don't know how dictionaries are made. Each new dictionary starts from scratch. The company making the dictionary employs thousands of "editors," to each of whom they give a list of words. The job of the editors is to collect as many examples as possible of the way in which these words *are actually used*. They look for the words in books, magazines, newspapers, and so forth, and every time they find one, they cut out or copy that particular example, building up a file of clippings where the words had been used. Then, reading these files, they decide *from the context* what the writer in each case had meant by the words. From these they make the definitions. A dictionary, in other words, is a collection of people's opinions about what words mean, as other people use them.

If I meet a new word, and cannot tell from the context what it means, it isn't true that I have gained nothing. I am like the dictionary editor—I have one example for the word. Next time I meet the word I will have another example, and so on. By the time I have met a word ten or twenty times I will almost certainly have a very good idea of its possible meanings.

For children reading (or adults, for that matter), the most important thing is *not* that they should understand all of what they read. No one does; what we get out of a piece of reading depends in large part on the experience we bring to it. What is important is that children should enjoy their reading enough to want to read more. The other thing that is important is that they should become better and better at getting meaning *from context*, for that is the supreme skill of a good reader. The trouble with telling children what words mean, or asking them to ask the dictionary to tell them, is that they don't get a chance to *figure out* the meaning of the word. Figuring out what you don't know or aren't sure of is the greatest intellectual skill of all.

Sensible Phonics

Years ago, a psychologist friend of mine, Robert Kay, told me about a very interesting way of teaching reading called Choral Reading. It was basically like the old "Sing Along with Mitch" TV show. The teacher would put on the board, in letters large enough for all the children to see, whatever they were going to read. Then she or he would move a pointer along under the words, and at the same time the children would read the words. The children who knew a word would read it; those who were not sure would perhaps read softly; those who didn't know at all would learn from those who were reading. No one was pointed out or shamed, all the children did as much as they could, and everyone got better.

Also many years ago, before the place became rich and stylish, my parents lived in Puerto Vallarta, Mexico. Now and then they used to visit a small elementary school not far from where they lived. The teacher taught reading through singing. The school was poor—now it is probably five times as rich, and has all the latest reading materials, and five times as many reading problems. The teacher wrote the words to a song on the board—perhaps a song that all the children knew, perhaps a new song that she taught them—and as she pointed at the words, the children sang them and, so doing, learned to read.

Any number of parents have told me a similar story: they read aloud to a small child a favorite story, over and over again. One day they find that as they read the child is reading with them, or can read without them. The child has learned to read simply by seeing words and hearing them at the same time. Though children who learn this way probably couldn't answer questions about it, *they have learned a great deal about phonics*. Nobody taught them to read, and they weren't particularly trying to learn. They weren't listening to the story *so that* they would be able to read later, but because it was a good story and they liked sitting on a comfortable grown-up lap and hearing it read aloud.

In many first-, second-, and third-grade classrooms I used to see signs on the walls—people tell me they are still up there—saying, "When two vowels go out walking, the first one does the talking." (Typical of the cutesy-wootsy way in which schools talk to young children.) What this means, of course is that there are many vowel pairs—bAIt, bEAt, bOAt, et cetera—in which the first of the two vowels makes the sound. OK to point that out to children, though the best way to do this would simply be to give examples. But the trouble with the cute little sentence that the schools have cooked up to tell children this is that *it* contains two vowel pairs, *both of which violate the rule*. This might not bother some children, either because they already understand what the rule is telling them or (more likely) because they don't *think* about anything they hear in school. But some children do think about what they see

21

and hear, and it is just such thoughtful and intelligent children who might very well be thrown for a loop by this dumb sentence on the wall.

Another confusing part of so-called phonics teaching is all the talk about "long" and "short" vowels. Among the sounds that vowels make is one that is the same as the *name* of the vowel, as in bAke, bEEt, and rOse. The schools have traditionally called these sounds the "long" vowel sounds. By contrast, they give the name "short" to the vowel sounds in bAck, bEt, bIt, and so on. Now, the fact is that there is nothing longer about the sound of *a* in bAke than its sound in bAck. We can say either word quickly or slowly, make either vowel sound as long or short as we wish. Again, calling one of these vowel sounds "long" and the other one "short," though it makes no sense—one might as well call one blue and the other green—might not bother the kind of children who (as I was) are ready to parrot back to the teacher whatever they hear, never mind what it means or whether it means anything. But it might be extremely confusing and even frightening to other kinds of children, including many of the most truly intelligent.

It might not even do any harm to call the sounds of bAck, bEt, and bIt "short" vowels, as long as we made it clear that there was nothing really any shorter about those sounds, and that we just used this word because we had to use *some* word, and people had been using this one for quite a while, so we decided we'd stick to it. After all, that's why we call dogs "dogs"; there is no particular sense to it, it's just that we've been doing it that way for a long time. But to say to children things that make no sense, *as if they did make sense*, is stupid and will surely cause some of them great and needless confusion.

These two small and perhaps not very damaging pieces of nonsense, and other much larger and more damaging ones that I will talk about next, were not invented and never would have been invented by parents teaching their own children. They were invented by people trying to turn a casual, natural, everyday act into a "science" and a mystery.

Let's now take a broader look at the teaching of reading, more specifically, what most people call "phonics." According to a newspaper report, a Board of Education "reading expert" in Chicago had made a list of 500 reading skills (later cut to 273) that children needed to learn in elementary school. What those lists could be made up of I cannot imagine and do not want to know. In a word, they are nonsense.

The fact is that there are only *two* general ideas that one needs to grasp in order to be able to read a phonic language like English (or French, German, and Italian, as opposed to, say, Chinese): (1) written letters stand for spoken sounds; (2) the order of the letters on the page, from our left to our right, corresponds to the order in time of the spoken sounds.

It is not necessary for children to be able to *say* these rules in order to understand and be able to use them. Nor is it a good idea to try to teach them these rules by saying and then explaining them. The way to teach them—that is, if you insist on teaching them—is to demonstrate it through very simple and clear examples.

Aside from that, what children have to learn are the connections between the 45 or so sounds that make up spoken English and the 380 or so letters or combinations of letters that represent these sounds in written English. This is not a large or a hard task. But, as in everything else, the schools do a great deal to make it larger and harder.

The first mistake they make is to teach or try to teach the children the sounds of each individual letter. In the case of consonants, this amounts to telling the children what is not true. Of the consonants, there are only six or seven that can be *said* all by themselves—*s* (or the *c* in niCe), *z* (or the *s* in riSe), *m*, *n*, *v*, *f*, *j* (or the *g* in George)—plus the pair *sh*. There are borderline cases of *l*, *r*, *w*, and *y*, but it seems wiser to let children meet these sounds in syllables and words. As for the rest, we cannot *say* the sounds that *b*, or *d*, or *k*, or *p*, or *t* make, all by themselves. *B* does *not* say "buh," nor *d* "duh." *Big* does not say "buh-ig," nor *rub* "ruh-buh." These letters don't make any sound, except perhaps the faintest puff of air, except when they are combined with a vowel in a word or syllable. Therefore, it is misleading and absurd, as well as false, to try to teach them in isolation.

It is equally foolish and mistaken to try to teach the vowel sounds in isolation, in this case because each vowel makes a number of different sounds, depending on what consonants it is combined with. Since we can't tell what the letter *a* says except as we see it joined with consonants, then it makes sense to introduce the sounds of *a* (or any other vowel) *only* in the context of words and syllables.

All we have to do then is to expose children to the two basic ideas of phonics: that written letters stand for and "make" spoken sounds, and that the order of the written letters matches the order of the spoken sounds. The first we can do very easily by any kind of reading aloud, whether of words in books, or signs, or whatever. The second we can do by writing down, and saying as we write them, words that use the six or seven consonants that we can sound alone, and so can stretch out in time. Thus we could write *Sam*, saying the *s* as we write the *s*, the *a* as we write it, and the *m* as we write it. Same with *man*, *fan*, *van*, or *mis*, or *us*, or *if*. It is neither necessary nor a good idea to be too thorough about this. It is not a lesson to be completely learned and digested the first or second time. That is not how children learn things. They have to live with an idea or insight for a while, turn it around in some part of their minds, before they can, in a very real sense, discover it, say "I see," take possession of the idea, and make it their own—and unless they do this, the idea will never be more than surface, parrot learning, and they will never really be able to make use of it.

Then, as children slowly take possession of these ideas about reading, we can introduce them to more words, and so more sounds, and the connection between the words and the sounds. While there are books such as the one I mentioned earlier (*Let's Read*) that list all of the one-syllable words that can be made from different combinations of consonants and vowels, it wouldn't take parents very long to make such lists for themselves—*bat*, *fat*, *cat*, *rat*, and so on. There is no need for such lists to be complete, just long enough to expose the child to the idea that words that look mostly alike will probably sound mostly alike.

In any case, hardly any children will want to spend much time with what are so obviously teaching materials. They will want to get busy reading (and writing) *real* words, words in a context of life and meaning. No need to talk here about ways to do that—people who read this are sure to have any ideas of their own. If we read and write, the children will want to; if we don't, they won't.

Another very common school mistake is to ask children to learn and memorize which letters are vowels and which are consonants. Schools usually do this by trying to teach the children some definitions of "vowel" and "consonant." These definitions are almost always inconsistent and self-contradictory, such as "A vowel is a sound that you can say all by itself." As I have said, this is equally true of some of the consonants. I have thought about this from time to time, and have never been able to think of a definition of vowels and consonants that was clear, distinct, and allowed no exceptions.

In any case, this is a bad way to teach children anything. They think best (as I suspect we all do) when they can move from the particular to the general. Beyond that, there is no good reason why children learning to read should learn the words "vowel" and "consonant." Knowing or not knowing those words has nothing whatsoever to do with reading.

I have written elsewhere about playing a game with children in which they ask me to write a word, and I write it. Next time I do this, I may use one colored pen to write the consonants, and another to write the vowels. Though I can imagine that some children, suspecting that I was trying to sneak in some teaching, might tell me not to do even that.

A better variation of that game might go like this. We could write each letter on a separate card or piece of paper, vowels in one color, consonants in another. Then we could say to the child, "Put together any two, or three, or four (or more) of these cards, and I will tell you what they say." If the child gave us *bsrx*, we could do our best to make those sounds. The child would begin to notice after a while that the only combinations of letters that made sounds that sounded like the words he heard around him were the ones that had both colors in them, and that these were very often in the form of consonant-color + vowel-color + consonant-color. If he ever asked, "What do you call this kind of letter, and what do you call this kind?" (I can't guess whether a child would be likely to do this), I would say, "We call these kinds of letters 'vowels' and these 'consonants.'" (If he asked why, I would tell him I didn't know.)

None of these tricks or games is necessary, or will

help a child to read faster or better. But for people who for whatever reasons feel they want to do *something*, I suggest these as things that might be fun (for both adult and child) to do, and, *as long as they are fun*, possibly useful, and probably not harmful.

How Not to Learn to Read

Leon, a young black man of about seventeen whom I met some years ago in an eastern city, was a student in an Upward Bound summer program. He was at the absolute bottom of all his regular school classes, tested, judged, and officially labeled as being almost illiterate. At the meeting I was part of, the students, some black, some white, all poor, had been invited to talk to their summer-school teachers about what they could remember of their own school experiences and how they felt about them. Until quite late in the evening Leon didn't speak. When he did, he didn't say much. But what he said I will never forget. He stood up, holding before him a paperback copy of Dr. Martin Luther King's book *Why We Can't Wait*, which he had read, or mostly read, during that summer session. He turned from one to another of the adults, holding the book before each of us and shaking it for emphasis, and, in a voice trembling with anger, said several times at the top of his lungs, "Why didn't anyone ever tell me about this book? Why didn't anyone ever tell me about this book?" What he meant, of course, was that in all his years of schooling no one had ever asked him to read, or ever shown him or mentioned to him, even one book that he had any reason to feel might be worth reading.

It's worth noting that *Why We Can't Wait* is full of long, intricate sentences and big words. It would not have been easy reading for more than a handful of students in Leon's or any other high school. But Leon, whose standardized Reading Achievement Test scores "proved" that he had the reading skills of a second-grader, had struggled and fought his way through that book in perhaps a month or so. The moral of the story is twofold: that young people want, need, and like to read books that have meaning for them, and that when such books are put within easy reach they will sooner or later figure out, without being "taught" and with only minimal outside help, how to read them.

In their book *On Learning to Read*, Bruno Bettelheim and Karen Zelan understand well and state eloquently the first half of this moral, but not the second. They argue about ways to improve the teaching, and miss the far more important point, that any teaching *that the learner has not asked for* is likely to impede and prevent his or her learning.

But in this I may misjudge them. Bettelheim is a most astute and realistic man, and it may be that, understanding the unwillingness of schools to make even simple changes in their ways of doing things, especially where doing this might require giving up the illusion that they can create and control all the learning of all the children, he and his colleague made a tactical decision to accept as given almost everything in the philosophy, organization, and practice of schools, and to concentrate their attention on two very limited targets: the abysmal lack of quality of the basal readers used in schools and the destructive ways in which teachers customarily respond to the mistakes children make when they read aloud in class.

With the first of these issues they are right on target. The books that most children are compelled to learn to read from are beyond belief boring, stupid, shallow, misleading, dishonest, and unreal. The figures alone tell the story:

> [The] first readers published in the 1920s contained on the average 645 different words. By the 1930s ... about 460 words. In the 1940s and 1950s ... about 350 words. [In] seven basic readers series published between 1960 and 1963 ... primer vocabularies [ranged from] 113 to 173 words.... In 1920 the number of running words per average story [in Scott, Foresman primers] was 333, by 1962 it had shrunk to 230.... The number of different words used in the entire book was 425 in 1920, 282 in 1930, 178 in 1940, and 153 in 1962.

Wondering why publishers keep restricting the vocabularies of their books, the authors say:

> One possible explanation ... is that as the readers became more boring, children learned to read less well. The conclusion drawn from this fact was not the obvious one that as textbooks became more boring to children and teachers alike, children would have a harder time working up an interest in learning to read. Instead, it was concluded that the books were too *difficult* for the children and that things should be made easier for them, by asking them to learn fewer words! So each new edition of a primer contains fewer words in ever more frequent repetition, and in consequence is more boring than that which preceded it.... As this cycle continues up to the present day, things have gone from bad to worse.

The badness of these readers is indeed a worthy target and may prove a vulnerable one. If only because it makes this point so strongly, Bettelheim and Zelan's book is well worth reading. And if to any degree it succeeds in reversing the downward cycle described above, and making readers more challenging, varied, interesting, and real, it will have been well worth the writing.

The largest part of *On Learning to Read* deals with the meanings of children's mistakes. The authors assert that it is wrong to assume that these mistakes are the result of ignorance and carelessness, and that the teacher's job is to correct them as quickly as possible, while criticizing or chastising the child for making them. Bettelheim and Zelan argue that these mistakes almost always have important meanings for the children. Teachers, they say, should understand this and let children know they understand. Beyond that, teachers should whenever possible figure out these hidden meanings and make them visible to the child, a process that suggests a kind of instant psychoanalysis.

Being experienced psychoanalysts themselves, Bettelheim and Zelan are dazzlingly ingenious at intuiting or ferreting out these hidden meanings. Do they never guess wrong? At least in the examples they cite, their understanding does indeed help the children to correct their mistakes, cope with their anxieties, make more sense of the text, and so progress in their reading. But Bettelheim and Zelan urge *all* teachers of reading to follow their example and use this method. I am not at all in sympathy with this part of their proposed remedy for the reading problem.

Paying such extraordinary attention to reading mistakes does work, but it seems roundabout, difficult, and in the end an unworkable solution to a problem that would not exist if the schools had not created it. Very few teachers are likely to be able to respond to children's mistakes in the patient, respectful, and thoughtful way Bettelheim and Zelan propose. They haven't the time, the training, and inclination, or, above all, the inherent sympathy and respect for children on which such work would have to rest. Indeed, I fear that in the unlikely event that the schools took this proposal seriously, the results would do more harm than good. There is far too much pseudopsychologizing and quack diagnosing of children in our schools as it is.

In any case, the problem this proposal aims to solve is wholly unnecessary. If teachers would only stop making children read aloud in class, they would not need to worry about how to respond to their mistakes. And, even more important, if children were allowed to read privately and for their own pleasure, they would soon catch and correct most of these mistakes themselves.*

How Not to Learn to Write: With Big Bird

From the point of view of education, learning, instruction, much of what I have seen on "Sesame Street," in the dozen or more times I have watched it, seems to me to be clumsy, misleading, and just plain wrong, typical of the worst things done in schools. This is a great pity. "Sesame Street," for example, puts great stress on the alphabet and on learning to count to ten or, more recently, twenty.

What we must do in helping anyone learn to read is to make very clear that writing is an extension of speech, that beyond every written word there is a human voice speaking, and that reading is the way to hear what those voices are saying. Like the schools, "Sesame Street" far too often blurs and hides these truths. That is all the more unfortunate, because TV can make the point more clearly and vividly than a teacher in a classroom. Suppose that children were to hear a voice speak-

* *New Boston Review* (March 1982).

31

ing and at the same time see the words, *as they are spoken*, appearing in print. Cartoon figures and the Muppets could have word balloons over their heads, as in comic strips, a convention that many children already know; even when live figures are speaking, the TV screen could be split, with the words appearing at the side—a TelePrompter in reverse.

Here is an example of something done extremely badly that might have been done well. Big Bird was standing by a wall on which he had put the letters OVEL. An adult came up, and Big Bird began to rhapsodize about the word he had put up, which he meant to be *love*. The adult told him that he did not have the word *love* on the wall, and as they discussed this, said that Big Bird's OVEL "did not spell anything." This statement could not be more false, or misleading, or damaging. The letters OVEL *do spell something*. They spell a word that anyone who can read can pronounce. The word doesn't happen to mean anything, but that is something else. Surely we have gotten past the Dick and Jane idea that you aren't reading a word unless you know its meaning. But then followed something worse. The adult began to say, in that typical teacher condescending-explaining, how-could-you-be-so-stupid voice, "But, Big Bird, you've put the *l after* the word, and you should have put it *before* it." She said this several times, as if it were self-evident that "before" meant "on the left side" and "after" meant "on the right side," and as if all she needed to do to make this clear was to say it often enough. In fact, there is nothing self-evident or natural or reasonable about it at all. We just do it that way. But nothing makes school more mysterious, meaningless, baffling, and terrifying to a child than constantly hearing adults tell him things as if they were simple, self-evident, natural, and logical, when in fact they are quite the reverse—arbitrary, contradictory, obscure, and often absurd, flying directly in the face of a child's common sense.

What might have been done instead? Here is one scenario. The adult reads OVEL aloud, "Oh-vell, oh-vell." He says, "What does that mean, Big Bird?" Big Bird says the word says "love." The adult insists it says "oh-vell." As other people come up, Big Bird appeals to each of them. They all read, "Oh-vell." From this we can see what is very important, that one of the advantages of written speech is that it says the same thing to everyone who can read it. . . . Anyway, after a number of people, adults and children, have told Big Bird that his word says "oh-vell," he says sadly that he wanted it to say "love." Then someone, preferably a child, says to him, "If you want it to say 'love,' all you have to do is put this *l* here." No nonsense about "before" and "after." Just move the letter. Then perhaps the child might say the word *love* slowly, moving his fingers under the letters matching the sounds. Big Bird might then say, "Oh, I see; the letters go that way." Note that even Big Bird's *mistake*, unlike most of the mistakes of children, was nonsensical. There would have been some reason to put EVOL on the wall, but not OVEL.

What is vital here, and in all reading, is the connection between the order *in time* of the sounds of the spoken word and the order *in space* of the letters of the written one. If so many children have trouble discovering this connection, it is because in most reading instruction we do so much to hide it—and this is no less true of the methods that, like "Sesame Street," make a big thing out of "What letter does the word begin with?"

On a program presented one day on the letter *x*, another opportunity was lost. An animated-cartoon narrator was trying to think of words that ended with *x*. First a fox went by, and the voice said "fox"—but the letters FOX did not appear on the screen. Then other words—*box, ox, ax*—with appropriate and clever pictures to match, but still no letters. Instead, we might have shown what Caleb Gattegno calls "transformations," the way the sound of a word changes when we change a letter in it—and it is making such transformations, not sounding out a word letter-by-letter, that good readers do when they meet words they don't know. Thus, beginning with FOX, we might have moved away from the *f* and brought in a *b* to make BOX, then removed the *b* to leave OX, then changed that to AX, and from there to TAX. We might then have brought in an *o* to make TOX. Here the cartoon narrator could have looked puzzled. "Tox? Tox?" he might have said. "I don't think there is any word such as *tox*. It is a nonsense word; some words you can say and write don't mean anything." Perhaps then a few more nonsense words. Perhaps a bit of business of looking up a word in a dictionary to see whether it has a meaning. Then perhaps back to FOX and from there to FIX.

As opposed to "capital letters," and in place of the exact word "lowercase," the show follows school in talking about "small" letters. This is nonsense. Whether a letter is a capital or not has nothing to do with size, but with shape. Indeed, the point should be made that a letter, capital or lowercase, can be as small or large as we care to make it. We might show writing on the head of a pin, big letters on a blackboard, children writing letters in the snow, skywriting.

A capital *A* is shown. A voice says that it is like an upside-down *V* with a line across. So far, so good. But why not show all the ways in which we can deform or change an *a* without losing its *a*-ness—make it taller, shorter, thicker, or more slender in the strokes, slanting left or right, and so on. Why not, with filmclips, show children many different shapes of *a*'s in real life? Why spread the false and absurd notion that there is only one way to make an *a*? Why not show children *making* many different shapes of *a*'s?

We might also find ways to reveal to children that all the writing they see around them began as someone speaking. With compressed time we could show very vividly the transition from spoken words to words written on signs or posters, where a great many people could see them. We might show a number of ways to write things, with pencil or pen or felt-tipped pen or typewriter, with ditto or mimeo, with printing, with electric signs, even with skywriting. We could show children tricks by which they could teach themselves to write.

In still other ways we could make clear to the children that writing is an extension of powers *they already have, and that they got for themselves*: namely, the powers of speech. We should constantly remind them that they figured out for themselves how to understand and talk like all the bigger people around them, and that learning to write and to read writing is easy. Writing is a kind of magic or deep-frozen speech, which the writer can use, day after day, to say to everyone who looks at it whatever he wants to say. It is an extension of the voice of the speaker, and since children sense their littleness and want to be larger and more potent, the idea that through writing they can make their voices reach much farther could be very exciting to them.*

Spelling

The best way to spell better is to read a lot and write a lot. This will fill your eye with the *look* of words, and your fingers with the *feel* of them. Good spellers

* *Atlantic Monthly* (May 1971).

do not look many words up in dictionaries, or memorize spelling rules. When they are not sure of how to spell a word, they spell it several ways and pick the one that looks best. In almost every case it turns out to be right. People who spell badly—I have taught many of them— are not much helped by rules and drills. In all my work as a teacher, nothing I ever did to help bad spellers was as effective as not doing *anything*, except telling them to stop worrying about it, and to get on with their reading and writing.

People who already spell somewhat badly would probably spell better if they taught themselves to type. Learing to type would make them *look* more carefully at words, and, as they concentrated on hitting the right keys they would, so to speak, build the proper spelling of these words into their fingers. It is often easier to build a new and correct habit into our neuromuscular system than to get an old incorrect one out.

But many will not agree with this, and will still insist that people can improve their own, or their children's, spelling by some kind of practice, drill, or testing. For them, here is a self-test for spelling, which enables students to keep track of which words they know and which they don't, and to work on the ones they don't.

On one side of a card we can print the word itself. Then, on the other side of the card, we need something to tell us what the word is without actually showing us the word, which would of course defeat the point of the test. I propose that we write each word on one side of a card, and on the other side write either (1) a picture that will tell what the word is and/or (2) a sentence or two in which the word is used, but the word itself is left blank.

Thus, to take a very simple example, a child writing a card for the word *horse* would write HORSE on one side (perhaps both in capitals and lowercase letters), and on the other side would draw a figure of a horse, or perhaps stick on a picture taken from a magazine. The child might also write a sentence about a horse, like "I want to ride a ———," or "My ——— eats hay," or "A colt is a young ———," and so on. It is important that those who will use the card draw the picture and/or make up the sentence(s); that way, they are much more likely to remember.

Then when the time comes to test themselves, the students can put the cards down, picture-side-up, take a card, look at the picture and read the sentence, figure out what the word is, spell it on another piece of paper, and then turn the card over to see whether they were right. The "right" cards could be put aside in one stack, the "wrong" cards in another. It would probably be good for students to go through their "wrong" cards again at the end of the test. The students themselves would decide how many words to try. People who are anxious about spelling would probably do better not to test themselves too long at a time. And it would probably be a good idea, whenever there got to be as many as, say, five cards in the "wrong" stack, for students to retest themselves on them before going on with other words.

Many words don't make pictures. Take "necessary," which many people misspell. In that case, on the reverse side of the card, instead of a picture, write something like "That's ne——y; I really need it." That will be enough to tell you what the word is, without giving away how to spell the hard part of the word. For "separate" you might write, "Don't put them together, keep them se——."

What is crucial in all this is that the *students* be in control of this testing and checking process. Just as it is better to let children make their own pictures, so it's better to let them make up their own definitions or examples; the ones they make up, they'll remember.

37

However useful this self-test might be, I beg, urge, and plead that you *not* do any of this with children just starting out to read and write. As I said, if they do plenty of reading and writing for pleasure, their spelling will improve as they get more and better word images in their minds. I would use this method only with children who had already become quite bad spellers.

One more question: Where would this list of words come from that the children would make up cards for? From one place *only*—misspelled words in their own writing. There could be no greater waste of time than asking children to learn to spell words that they are not *using*.

This method would work just as well for adults.

Handwriting

When I was little I was taught cursive handwriting, found it easy and pleasant to do, and soon developed a small and fairly neat handwriting that, at least when I am being careful, has not changed much to this day.

Teaching fifth grade, and seeing many students with slow, tortured, scrawly, irregular "cursive" writing, I began to wonder why the schools insisted on teaching cursive. Still believing then that schools had good reasons for everything they did, I decided it must be because cursive writing was so much faster than manuscript printing. Since my own handwriting, particularly when I was using it a lot, was very small and quick, I could easily believe this. Secretly I thought that probably very few people could write as fast as I could.

One day in fifth grade I told my students about "The quick brown fox jumps over the lazy dog," the famous typing sentence (one of many, I later learned) that contains all the letters of the alphabet. I asked them to see how many times they could write it in a half-minute, which I timed with a stopwatch. After each trial, they counted up the number of words they had written, to see how much they improved with practice. We did a number of things like this in the class, in which students competed not against others but themselves, trying to break their own records. The children enjoyed these contests in which, since everybody improved, everybody won. They fell to work with a will on "the quick brown fox"—as I did, sitting at my desk, racing along with my tiny handwriting.

When I began walking around the room looking at the papers, which the children eagerly stuck in my face to show their improvement, I received a shock. Three of them could apparently write faster than I could, even though they used manuscript printing, one sloppily but two quite neatly. I thought, "This can't be right, there must be a mistake somewhere, I must have counted wrong, these ten-year-olds can't possibly write fat manuscript letters faster than my itty-bitty superspeedy cursive." I proposed we write some more quick brown foxes. They gladly agreed. Back at my desk, I made my pen *fly*. This time we would see! Alas, the results were the same—I was still the fourth fastest writer in the class. (Did I confess? I don't remember.)

So why do we teach and demand cursive writing in schools? I have no idea. Pure habit, I guess. In the words of the old song, "Do, do, do what you done, done, done before." Later I learned that school cursive, called in my day Palmer penmanship, had evolved from an elaborate decorative script invented for engraving in copper, a very slow and painstaking form of writing that had nothing to do with speed. Someone, somewhere, decided that it would be nice if children learned to write like copperplate engraving, and the rest, as they say, is history.

The other day I decided to test these two types of writing myself, to see whether I could write faster in cursive or in the modified italic manuscript print that I sometimes use to write little notes in my office. I found to my surprise that though I have been using cursive writing all my life, and until making this test had been doing much more writing than printing, *I* could print faster than I could write. The difference was not very great, but it was consistent. No matter how much I warmed up and practiced my cursive, I could never make it as fast as my printing.

Why should this be so? The only reason I can think of is that when we move from the end of one letter to the beginning of another, we can move our pen a little bit faster through the air than across the paper, partly because the paper slows down the pen a tiny bit, and partly because when we move our pen through the air we don't have to worry about what the joins or connections between the letters look like.

So, at the tender age of fifty-seven, I am going to drop cursive (except for my signature) and do all my pen and pencil writing in my modified print. Since it is both faster and more legible, why not?

Why, in general, is print more legible than cursive writing? Or, to put it a little differently, why are unjoined letters easier to read than joined? Because there is no possibility of confusing the joins ("ligatures," as one italics book calls them) with the letters themselves. This is one of the main problems of most illegible handwriting; you often can't tell whether a particular mark on the paper is part of a letter or only a join between letters.

So now we have two solid and convincing reasons

for resisting, if we want to, the demand of the schools that our children learn cursive writing—print is more legible, and is demonstrably faster. Of course, if children want to learn cursive writing, because they like the way it looks, or because they see some grown-up doing it, they can. But there is no sensible reason to make them.

Only a few basic shapes and pen strokes are needed to make letters, and all these pen strokes are easily and quickly made by the hand and fingers. On the whole, I see no reason to make children waste time practicing these shapes. If they write, as they speak, in order to say things they want to say to people they want to say them to, and if they have good models of printing to look at, they will improve their writing just as they improve their speech. A possible exception—children who have learned to write cramped, awkward, illegible cursive may need *a little* practice on shapes just to loosen up their hands and give them the feeling that printing can feel as well as look good. But I wouldn't push this if a child resisted, preferring to write *real* writing: that is, writing meant for others to read.

Citizen in the World of Books

As I write this, Helen (ten months old) is sitting in the doorway to my office with a paperback book, *The Land of Oz*, in her hands. She is having a fine time with it. For her it is mostly a shiny rectangular object, just thick enough to get a good grip on and wave around, except that because of its shiny cover it slips out of her hands easily and lands every so often with a nice thump on the floor. Now and then she will get hold of it by the cover alone, but she has not discovered, for the most part, that a book is made up of a lot of separate thin pages that can be turned, torn, crumpled, looked at, or whatever.

Just yesterday, her sister Anna (three) was sitting in a big armchair holding a book, *A. J. Wentworth, B.A.*, from which she was reading to her mother, Mary, seated beside her. What Anna was saying *sounded* very much like reading; she had a reading "tone" in her voice. But the words, instead of having to do with A. J. Wentworth, were all about the adventures of some imaginary friends of hers. Seeing me looking at her from the doorway, Anna interrupted herself to say something like "I'm reading this book to Mama, and I'm reading the words." I said, "Yes, I can hear that," and after listening a bit more, went on about my business. Later, Mary told me that quite often Anna would stop "reading" right in the middle of a sentence of her story, turn the page, and go on, just like someone really reading from a book.

Watching and listening to her, and watching her baby sister today, made me realize there are two diametrically opposite ways of opening to children the world of books. One way is to start them with the names and sounds of individual letters, then with small words, then with small groups of these words joined to make small sentences, then with small reading books, and then other books, each a little harder than the one before, until the children supposedly have enough reading skills to read any book they want. The trouble is that by this time most of them wouldn't care if they never saw another book in their lives. Gaining entry into the world of books this way boils down to surmounting a long row of obstacles, each a little larger than the one before, or going through a series of locked doors that open only when you say the correct password, only to lead you, of course, to still another locked door.

The other way of opening the world of books to children is the way it has been done for Anna. The world of books was first opened to her, she became a citizen of it, when for the first time she clutched a book in her hand and thought, "This book is *mine!*" Instead of beginning with a tiny idea, the sound of a letter, she began with a big and important one, that books belong to people and could belong to her. In time she filled in this big idea with smaller but still large ideas: that books have stories locked in them, that they have written words in them, and that the stories are somehow contained in the words, so that somehow figuring out the words is the key to unlocking and taking possession of the stories, and that these stories can be shared with, given to, other people.

Your conventionally taught child, even when much older than Anna, may know nothing of books except how to figure out what the words say. *Anna knows everything else about books*, including all the important things.

At Home with Numbers

I suspect that many children
would learn arithmetic, and learn
it better, if it were illegal.

Counting

When my niece was four or five, her older brothers and sisters taught her to count, "Sesame Street" style, by having her recite the names of the numbers in order. I heard her say, "One, two, three, four, seven, six, eight," at which point I heard the indignant voices of a couple of the other kids saying to her, "No! No! Seven comes *after* six!"

It occurred to me then, and many times since, that from such talk children could get a very strange notion about numbers. They might see them as a procession of little creatures, the first one named One, the second named Two, the third Three, and so on. Later on these tiny creatures would seem to do mysterious and meaningless dances, about which people would say things like "Two and two make four." It seemed likely that any child with such a notion of numbers could get into serious trouble before long, and this did indeed happen to my niece. Some years later I asked several adults who themselves had always been hopeless in arithmetic what they thought of this notion of mine, and many of them laughed and said that this was indeed the feeling they had always had about numbers and was part of the reason why they had always had such trouble with them.

For this reason it seems to me extremely important that children not be taught to count number names in the absence of real objects. No doubt first-grade teachers like to have their children able to say, "One, two, three," but this ability has nothing necessarily to do with an understanding of numbers.

To put it differently, when little children first meet numbers they should *always* meet them as adjectives, not nouns. It should not at first be "three" or "seven," all by itself, but always "two coins" or "three matches" or "four spoons" or whatever it might be. There is time enough later, probably much later, for children to intuit the notion that the noun "five" is that quality that all groups of five objects have in common.

I would say, too, that it is not at all necessary, and indeed not a good idea, to have children meet numbers always in the counting order. Thus, we might at one moment show a child two of some kind of object, but the next thing we show, according to the circumstances, might be five of some other object, or eight, or whatever. Numbers exist in nature in quite random ways, and children should be ready to accept numbers, so to speak, where they find them.

It would also be helpful, at least some of the time, to have children see, and in time learn to recognize, some of the smaller numbers, probably everything smaller than ten, by the sorts of patterns they make. Thus, a child shown three small objects might on one occasion see them in a row, on another, see them arranged in a triangle. Four objects could be shown, either arranged in a square, or in a row of three with another one on top. The patterns for five could be a regular pentagon, or a square with another one on top, as in the manner of a child's drawing of a house, or perhaps a square with another object in the center. Six we could show in two rows of three, or a triangle with a row of three on the bottom, then two, then one, or perhaps in other ways. Such patterns might be put on cards, perhaps with the number symbol or digit of the card on the other side. I'm not for one moment suggesting that children should be forced, or even encouraged, to memorize these cards. But if such cards were available for children to see and play with in various ways, perhaps to play matching games with, they might intuit and in a short time come to learn these relationships. It seems to me important for a child to have ways *other* than counting to identify small numbers.

In this connection, a set of dominoes might be a useful toy, and indeed I would guess that quite young children would enjoy playing dominoes even if they could do no more than match patterns with other patterns. Questions of scoring could come in later.

It also seems to me important that if and when adults are counting objects for a child, that they *not* move from one object to the next, saying as they go, "One, two, three." The child, seeing the adult touching these items, which in other respects all look exactly alike, and saying a different word for each one, may very well conclude that in some strange way "one, two, three" are the names of these objects. This confusion can be easily avoided. As we count each item we can move it over to one side, saying at the first, "Now we have one," then, as we move the second object to it, "Now we have two," and then in turn, "Now there are three, now there are four, now five," and so on. Thus at every point the number name refers not to a particular object but to the size of the group of objects that we have set to one side.

Somewhere along the line we could introduce the idea of ordinal numbers: that is, the numbers that indicate the *place* of an item in an array, and not the size of a group of items. Thus, given a row of small objects, we might touch them in turn, saying as we go something like "This is the first one; this is the second one, and the third one, and the fourth one, and the fifth, and the sixth." There is no need at first to talk about such notions as "cardinal" and "ordinal." If we simply use words in a way that reflects the nature of these ideas, the child will in a fairly short time grasp the difference.

When we are counting a number of small objects, there is no necessity that we should always count by ones. We might just as well move two objects over to the side at a time, saying as we do, "Now we have two, now four; now we have six," or in some cases we might count by threes or fours or whatever, gradually getting across to the child that there are many ways of doing this and that we can pick the one that seems most handy.

Some children, of course, grasp these notions of cardinal and ordinal in spite of our rather confusing way of presenting them, and often in spite of our own confusions, but many do not, and I strongly suspect that a great many children might find it easier to understand these distinctions if, when we first introduce them, we use methods such as these.

Addition and Subtraction

Sometime during first grade most children will be told, and asked to write down and to memorize, that $2 + 3 = 5$. This may be called a "number fact," or an "addition fact," or both. The children will almost certainly be given a list of such facts to memorize and repeat on demand. Their books and teachers will explain and illustrate this fact in different ways, such as showing a picture of two baby chicks, then one of three baby chicks, then one of five baby chicks, or some other "cute" thing that children are supposed to like.

Another "number fact" that the children will be told is that $3 + 2 = 5$. They will almost always hear it as a separate fact, not connected with the fact $2 + 3 = 5$. Some children will wonder why the two number facts come out the same. Once in a great while, one of them will ask why. Some teachers may answer, "They just do, that's all." Less old-fashioned teachers may reply, "Because addition is commutative." This is just putting a big mystery in place of a little one. Even a child who understood what "commutative" meant might say, "I can *see* that it's commutative; what I want to know is, *why* is it?" But children generally don't say things like that, they just slump back in their seats thinking, "One more thing that makes no sense."

Before long the children will be told two new "number facts" or "subtraction facts." One is that $5 - 2 = 3$, the other, that $5 - 3 = 2$. Again, they will hear these as separate facts, not connected with each other or with the addition facts they met in first grade. Again, their teachers and textbooks will give various explanations of what subtraction "means." In one "good school" I taught in, there was a near civil war about this. One group of teachers wanted to say that $5 - 3 = 2$ means, or can mean, "What do we have to add to 3 in order to get 5?" This is how people count change in stores—they begin with the amount of your purchase, then add change and bills to it to equal the amount of money you gave them. It is a perfectly sensible method. But the other faction in this school, including the head of the lower-school math department, denounced this as "additive subtraction," and told the elementary teachers that they must not use *or allow the children to use* this way of thinking about subtraction. He said they must think only in terms of "taking away."

Meanwhile, there are children struggling in the face of growing anxiety (theirs and their teachers') to memorize all these disconnected and meaningless facts, as if they were learning the words to a song in a language they did not know. After a year or so some children become good at parroting back number facts, but most don't know them and never will—they have already joined the giant army of people who "can't do math."

None of this is necessary.

$2 + 3 = 5$, $3 + 2 = 5$, $5 - 2 = 3$, and $5 - 3 = 2$ are not four facts, but four different ways of looking at *one* fact. Furthermore, that fact is not a fact of arithmetic, to be taken on faith and memorized like nonsense syllables. It is a fact of nature, which children can discover for themselves, and rediscover or verify for themselves as many times as they need or want to.

The fact is this:

$$***** \leftrightarrow *** **$$

If you have before you a group of objects—coins or stones, for example—that looks like the group on the left, then you can make it into two groups that look like the ones on the right. Or—and this is what the two-way arrow means—if you have two groups that look like the ones on the right, you can make them into a group that looks like the one on the left.

This is not a fact of arithmetic, but a fact of *nature*. It did not become true only when human beings invented arithmetic. It has nothing to do with human beings. It is true all over the universe. One doesn't have to know any arithmetic to discover or verify it. An infant playing with blocks or a dog pawing at sticks might do that operation, though probably neither of them would notice that he had done it; for them, the difference

51

between ***** and *** ** would be a difference that didn't make any difference. Arithmetic began (and begins) when human beings began to notice and think about this and other numerical facts of nature.

Early in human history people began to invent special names to talk about that property of a group of objects that had to do only with how many objects there were. Thus, a group of five kittens, a group of five shoes, and a group of five apples have in common only that there are the same number in each group, so that for each kitten there would be one shoe or one apple, with none left over. And it is a property of the number 5 that it can be separated into the two smaller numbers 2 and 3. It is another property of 5 that it can be separated into 4 and 1. And it is still another property of 5 that these are the *only* two ways in which it can be separated into two smaller numbers. If we start with 7, we can get 6 and 1, or 5 and 2, or 4 and 3; with 10 we can get 9 and 1, 8 and 2, 7 and 3, 6 and 4, or 5 and 5. Every number can be split into two smaller numbers in only a certain number of ways—the bigger the number, the more ways. (There is a regular rule about this, a simple one, which children—and adults—might enjoy finding for themselves.)

Once we get it clear in our minds that ***** = *** ** is a fact of nature, we can see that $3 + 2 = 5$, $2 + 3 = 5$, $5 - 2 = 3$, and $5 - 3 = 2$, whether we put these in symbols or in words (such as "plus," "added to," or "take away"). *They are simply four different ways of looking at and talking about one original fact.*

What good is this? The good is that instead of having dozens of things to memorize, we have only four, and those all sensible. Once children can turn ***** = *** ** into $3 + 2 = 5$ or any of the other forms, they can look at any other number, find out how it may be split into two parts, and then write down all the ways of talking about that.

Thus a child might take ********, find out by experiment that it could be split (among other ways) into ****** and **, and then write down 6 + 2 = 8, 2 + 6 = 8, 8 − 2 = 6, and 8 − 6 = 2, and then do the same with 7 and 1, or 5 and 3, or 4 and 4. In short, all the number facts that children are now *given*, and then asked to memorize, they could discover and write down *for themselves*. The advantage of the latter is that our minds are much more powerful when discovering than memorizing, not least of all because discovering is more fun. Another advantage is that so much of arithmetic (and by extension mathematics) that now seems mysterious and full of coincidences and contradictions would be seen to be perfectly sensible.

Once, when I talked about this to some teachers, one man said that his school was already teaching addition this way. It turned out that what he meant is that in their textbooks, for every "number fact," 3 + 4 = 7, for example, there was an illustration of four baby chicks, three baby chicks, and seven baby chicks (or whatever). But this completely missed the point I was trying to make, and am making here. ** *** = ***** is *not* an illustration of the fact 2 + 3 = 5. ** *** = ***** *is* the fact, and 2 + 3 = 5 only one of a number of ways of talking about it and putting it in symbols.

A Homemade Adding Machine

When children are first learning to add and subtract, they don't need anything as fancy as a calculator to help them work more quickly. We can make for children, or show them how to make, a simple adding and subtracting "machine" out of two rulers, or even out of two pieces of paper marked off like rulers.

Suppose we have two rulers or pieces of paper like this:

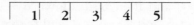

Here's how we use them to add 4 + 3. We put the left-hand end of one rule against the 4 mark on the other, like this:

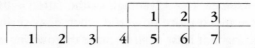

Then we look at the 3 mark on the second ruler, and we see that it is against the 7 mark on the first ruler. This shows us that 4 + 3 = 7. Though not all children might see this at first, it is clear that by using our rulers this way we have added a 4-unit length to a 3-unit length to make a 7-unit length. If our rulers are long enough, we can do this with any two numbers.

Children using this cheap adding machine may soon notice some things that rote memorization would never reveal. One would be that when, as in our figure, the left end of one ruler is against the 4 on the other, we can see just by looking at the ruler that:

$$4 + 1 = 5$$
$$4 + 2 = 6$$
$$4 + 3 = 7$$
$$4 + 4 = 8, \text{ and so on.}$$

In other words, each time we increase by 1 the number we are adding to 4, our answer increases by 1. This may seem simple enough to those of us who know it, but it isn't simple to a lot of school-taught children, even those who "know their addition facts." Many of these children might know very well, for example, that

$6 + 6 = 12$, but might have to struggle hard to "remember" what $6 + 7$ equaled. Plenty of them would get it wrong—I have seen it myself many times.

The first time a child discovers that when you add 1 to one of two numbers being added together, you make your answer 1 bigger, it is an exciting discovery, and no less important just because many people know it already. Later on the child might discover that when you add 2 to one of two numbers you are adding together, it makes your answer 2 bigger. More excitement. And the same is true for 3, or 4, and so on.

In algebra, we would write our discovery:

$$x + (y + a) = (x + y) + a$$

But I don't think I would tell this to a young child, unless he or she were already familiar with the idea that x or y could stand for any number. This, by the way, is probably an idea that most six-year-olds can grasp faster than most ninth-graders—at least, ninth-graders who have had eight years of school math.

If we use yardsticks or meter sticks, or simply make paper or cardboard rules 40 or 50 units long, or longer, children may notice many more things, such as this sequence and others like it:

$$4 + 3 = 7$$
$$14 + 3 = 17$$
$$24 + 3 = 27$$
$$34 + 3 = 37, \text{ and so on.}$$

Again, I have known plenty of school-taught children for whom $4 + 3$, $14 + 3$, $24 + 3$, and $34 + 3$ were completely different problems. They might say that $4 + 3 = 7$ and then turn around and say that $24 + 3 = 29$, or something even more ridiculous. This is what happens when people teach arithmetic as a pile of disconnected facts to be memorized. Children have no sense of the logic or order of numbers against which they can check their memory, or that they can use if their memory is uncertain.

Abstractions

I have often heard it said that numbers are abstract and must be taught abstractly. People who say this do not understand either numbers or abstractions and abstract-ness. Of course numbers are abstract, but like any and all other abstractions, they are an abstraction *of something*. People invented numbers to help them memorize and record certain properties of reality—numbers of animals, boundaries of an annually flooded field, observations of the stars, the moon, the tides, and so on. These numbers did not get their properties from people's imaginations, but from the things they were designed to represent. A map of the United States is an abstraction, but it looks the way it does not because the mapmaker wanted it that way, but because of the way the United States looks. Of course, mapmakers can and must make certain choices, just as did the inventors of numbers. They can decide that what they want to show on their maps are contours, or climate, or temperature, or rainfall, or roads, or air routes, or the historical growth of the country. Having decided that, they can decide to color, say, the Louisiana Purchase blue, or red, or yellow—whatever looks nice to them. But once they have decided what they want to map, and how they will represent it, by colors, or lines, or shading, reality then dictates what the map will look like.

The same is true with numbers. Down the line it may be useful to consider numbers and the science of working with them without any reference to what they stand for, just as it might be useful to study the general science of mapping without mapping any one place in particular. But it is *illogical, confusing, and absurd* to start there with young children. The only way they can become familiar with the idea of maps, symbol systems, abstractions of reality, is to move from known realities to the maps or symbols of them. Indeed, we all work this way. I know how contour maps are made—in that sense I understand them; but I cannot do what my brother-in-law, who among other things plans and lays out ski areas, can do. He can look at a contour map and instantly, in his mind's eye, feel the look and shape of the area. The reason he can do this while I can't is that he has walked over dozens of mountains and later looked at and studied and worked on the contour maps of areas where he was walking. No amount of explanation will enable any of us to turn an unfamiliar symbol system into the reality it stands for. We must go the other way first.*

Multiplication

Just as they are given lists of unrelated "addition facts" and "subtraction facts" to memorize in first and second grades, so most children, when they reach third grade, will begin to meet "multiplication facts." One such fact would be that $2 \times 3 = 6$, another that $3 \times 2 = 6$. If children ask about this coincidence, they may well be told, as they were about addition, that "multiplication is commutative," which of course explains nothing, just tells them in fancier and more mysterious words what they already knew. They will almost certainly be given a list of "100 multiplication facts" to memorize and will be tested on these often. Still later,

* An earlier version of these passages on abstraction appeared in *What Do I Do Monday* (New York: Dell, 1970).

probably in fifth grade, they will begin to meet fractions, and will be told that $\frac{1}{2} \times 6$ (sometimes "one-half of six") = 3 and that $\frac{1}{3} \times 6 = 2$. Still later, they may be told that 2 and 3 are factors of 6.

So, somewhere between first or second and about seventh grade (depending on which standard arithmetic texts their teachers have been ordered to use) the children will have collected (complete with explanations, and illustrations of baby chicks and pieces of pie) these more or less unrelated facts connected with the number 6:

$$2 \times 3 = 6$$
$$3 \times 2 = 6$$
$$6 \div 2 = 3$$
$$6 \div 3 = 2$$
$$\tfrac{1}{2} \times 6 = 3$$
$$\tfrac{1}{3} \times 6 = 2$$
$$6 \times \tfrac{1}{2} = 3$$
$$6 \times \tfrac{1}{3} = 2$$

2 is one-third of 6

3 is one-half of 6

2 and 3 are factors of 6

But, as I said about "addition facts," these are not separate "multiplication facts" or "division facts" or whatever. They are *one* fact, a fact not of arithmetic but of nature, a natural property of the number 6, which children can find for themselves and verify as often as they need or want to. The fact is that when you have this many objects:

******

you can arrange them like this:

***
***

All those "facts" written out above are simply different ways of writing down and talking about this one fact. So anyone, having discovered this property or fact about 6, and having been told the different ways in which we write and talk about this fact, could look for and find similar facts about other numbers, and then use those same ways of writing them down.

People (young or old) who do this will find that there are some numbers (2, 3, 5, 7, et cetera) that they cannot arrange in more than one row and have the rows come out even. They might be interested in knowing that we call such numbers "prime" and all other numbers "composite." One of a number of properties of any and every whole number is that it is either prime or composite. Some people might be interested in finding out for themselves what some of the prime numbers are, say, up to 200, or in learning that, using modern computers, people have been able to list all the primes up to some very large number, or that no one has yet found a formula that he or she can prove will generate all the prime numbers.

I am not saying that what I have written above about properties of 6 and our ways of saying and writing them are things that every child should know, or parents must be sure to tell their children. I suspect that what I have said about reading, that more children would learn it, and learn it better, if it were illegal, is just as true of elementary arithmetic. And there are many people who are right now leading interesting, useful, satisfying lives who do not know any arithmetic at all. On the other hand, what I have said about numbers here seems to me interesting, and useful in many circumstances. Other things being anywhere equal, I would rather know it than not know it.

In any case, if we are going to show and/or tell children about multiplying, dividing, fractions, factors, and so on, we would do well to do it more or less as shown above, so that those different ideas of arithmetic are connected from the *very beginning*.

Those Easy Tables

Although many happy and successful adults couldn't recite the multiplication tables to save themselves, it's handy to know them. If we approach them right, they are easy to know, and the patterns they make are exciting for children to discover.

It is important to think in terms of "knowing" the tables, not "learning" them. And the best way to know them is *not* to sit down and try to memorize them, one at a time, like words in some strange language, but to become familiar with them, to see how they work, and to use them. After a while we find that we know them without ever having consciously learned them—just as we know many thousands of words in our native language without ever having "learned" any of them. Without being aware of the process, we have become friends with them.

Here's a way to become familiar with the multiplication tables that will make them easier and more fun to know, that will make them stick better in memory, that will offer something to fall back on when memory is not sure, and that will give some idea of how numbers work, and the beauty and harmony in the patterns they make.

We begin with a 10 × 10 grid, ten rows of squares, ten squares in each row. Number the rows 1 to 10 down the side, and columns 1 to 10 across the top. Every square in the grid will be in a numbered row and a numbered column. To fill out the grid you put in each square the product of the number of the row it is in, and the number of the column.

	1	2	3	4	5	6	7	8	9	10
1										
2			6							
3										
4					20					
5										
6										
7		14								
8										
9										
10										

The drawing shows the basic grid with a few of these products filled in. For the square in the 2 row and the 3 column, the number we want to put inside is the product 2 × 3, or 6. In the square in the 4 row and the 5 column, we want the product 4 × 5, or 20. And so on. If you yourself don't feel at home with the tables, I'd suggest you fill in an entire grid yourself, taking as much time as you want. Use a calculator if you like.

One way to start children working on tables is to start out with an empty grid and have them slowly fill it in. Give them plenty of time to do this—weeks or even months, if need be. The grid might be posted in some convenient place—the refrigerator door, for example—so that as children figure out a new product they can put it in its proper square. But there's no rush. What will probably happen is what we hope will happen—the children will probably first fill in the 1 and 2 rows and columns, and then the 5 rows and columns, and the 10 rows and columns. They will think of these products as being "easy." Perfect! When they think of a product as being easy they *already* know it, probably so securely that they will never forget it.

Suppose, in filling out these squares, a child makes a mistake. Don't correct it; leave it alone. As children get more familiar with the tables and the patterns they make, they will see that one of the numbers looks wrong, doesn't seem to fit, causes contradictions—just as children teaching themselves to read see these kinds of contradictions when they read a word wrong. What is far more important than knowing the tables as such is that children should feel that numbers behave in orderly and sensible ways. Children who feel this, when they do make a mistake, can usually say, "Wait a minute; that doesn't make sense," and find and correct the mistake.

At any rate, at some point the child will put all the products in the grid. If the grid is on the refrigerator door or in some other visible place, filling in the last square will be quite exciting. There might even be a little ceremony.

Of course, if there is a calculator around, the child who knows how to use it will be able to fill in the grid very quickly. Fine. Even in filling out the grid this way the child will begin to notice some of the patterns. The game may then become, How much of the grid can I fill out without using the calculator? Please don't ask, "How much can you remember?" Most of what children know, they don't "remember"—that is, they aren't conscious of remembering—and if we start them worrying about what they can remember and what they can't, we will simply make more and more of their knowledge unavailable to them.

Without wanting to turn these suggestions into exact rules, I'd suggest that when the first grid has been filled out, correctly or incorrectly, you take it down from its public place and put up a new blank grid. The child will fill this out more quickly than the first one. More products will seem easy than happened the first time. If mistakes were made the first time, some or all of them will be noticed and corrected. But even if the same mistake keeps turning up, don't worry. Sooner or later the child will catch and correct it.

Here are some variations of the grid-filling game. (1) When children can fill in an entire grid in, say, less than five minutes, let them do it against the clock and see how long it takes. Next time, see if they can do it a little faster—children like breaking their own "records." (2) See how many products the child can fill in in a given time, say one or two minutes. The child will stay away from the "hard" products, will race through the products that are already easy, and will spend the most time thinking about those products that used to be hard and that are now beginning to be easy. One day a child will have to think a few seconds to figure that $5 \times 6 = 30$. A few days later the child will know it—that product will have become easy—and will move to other semi-hard products, which will in their turn become easy, until one day *all* are easy. (3) Try filling out the grid backward: that is, begining with the lower right-hand corner, going up each column and left along each row. Children doing this will see new patterns they hadn't noticed—as you go up the 9's column, the last digit goes up 1 each time, and so on. (4) Make a grid with the columns and rows numbered randomly, and see how long it takes to fill that out. (This is harder.)

Even the amount of drill we have just described is probably unnecessary. The best way for children to come to know the multiplication tables is by discovering the ways in which they relate to each other and the kinds of patterns they make. Thus, children who can multiply by 2 and by 3 have a way to figure out almost all of the tables. Why waste a lot of time memorizing what you know you can quickly figure out? And in any case, children who have figured out half a dozen times what a particular product is will probably remember it next time it comes up.

Yet, many of us, as I mentioned, have found the tables handy to know. Years ago, when teaching math, I tried various ways to make learning them more interesting and exciting. When learning is exciting, children learn the most. The following is a memo I wrote at the time:

> The trouble with almost all kinds of arithmetic drill is that they either bore children or scare them. The result is that either children learn nothing in the first place or that their learning is so unpleasant that they quickly forget it.

> I have been working with a few third graders who, though bright about numbers in many ways, have been weak on multiplication tables, which makes the school anxious. It occurred to me one day that I remember telephone numbers more by the way they sound than by the way they look, and therefore, that the old-fashioned way of memorizing by verbal repetition might help the children, if I could jazz it up a bit. The trick would be to engage their full attention without making them anxious.

> After a while I hit on something that seemed to work quite well. I began by putting on the board a grid of all the products of the numbers 6 through 9, like this:

	6	7	8	9
6	36	42	48	54
7	42	49	56	63
8	48	56	64	72
9	54	63	72	81

> The children have worked with these grids, and know that the square which is, for example, in the 6 row and the 7 column should be filled in with the product of 6 and 7. I used 6 through 9 because these are the tables

that children think are "hardest" and on which they have the most trouble.

I began with the products filled in, as shown. I had some kind of pointer in each hand. I explained to the children that if I put one of the pointers against, say, the 7 at the left side, and the other against, say, the 9 on top, they were to say "seven nines are sixty-three," and so on. We began. As I moved the pointers around, I could tell by the slowness of their answers that they were having to look for each product. But gradually, as they became more confident, they began to answer more and more quickly, without having to look for the product, or perhaps knowing instantly where to find it.

At this point I had a sudden idea or inspiration, and made a change that made the game more interesting. I erased one of the products in the squares. All the children exclaimed at this. I made a point of asking them that product as soon as I had erased it, and quite frequently thereafter, so that it would get a chance to stick. The children were surprised and pleased to find that they did remember that product, even when it "was not there." Whether they remembered mostly the sound of their own voices saying the product, or what it had looked like when it was written in, I don't know; I didn't think to ask them. Perhaps it is as well I did not; if they had had to think about *how* they remembered, I might have jarred the memory loose from their subconscious, and they might have stopped remembering.

As time went on I erased more and more products, first in the 6 row and then in the others. The children became more and more excited and interested as the number of blank squares increased, and as they found to their great astonishment that they really could remember what they could no longer see.

The time came when none of them could remember a product that belonged in one of the blank squares. When this happened, I said nothing, but simply wrote the product back in. This caused further excitement, and cries of "I knew it was that!" By the time there were only two or three products left in the grid, the children had turned this exercise into a contest in which they tried to see whether they could get all the squares blanked out before they failed to remember a product. At one point I asked for a product that none of them knew. I took the chalk and started to write it in, but before my hand reached the board one of them shouted the correct answer, and they all began to shout, "You can't write it in, you can't write it in!" I agreed this was only fair. Soon all the squares were blank and they had won the game.

I have no further notes on this subject, so I guess that multiplication tables were soon no longer a problem for us, or at any rate, that I soon stopped seeing them as such. But this might well be a game—it reminds me a little of the card game "Concentration," which children love and are good at—that children could play with adults or each other. Those who found the game interesting could of course make it more so by adding more tables, such as the 11 and 12 and perhaps still others.

Multiplying Large Numbers

Our ways of multiplying multiplace numbers, 24 × 57 or 132 × 853, for example, all depend on a simple fact about numbers. We could say it like this: if two numbers, let's say 3 and 5, add up to another number, in this case 8, then 2 times 8 is equal to 2 times 3 added to 2 times 5.

We can write this:

$$2 \times 8 = (2 \times 3) + (2 \times 5)$$

But some people are puzzled about why this should be

so. Or maybe they can see that it is so for small numbers:

$$3 \times 14 = (3 \times 10) + (3 \times 4)$$
$$= \quad 30 \quad + \quad 12$$
$$= \quad 42$$

But they aren't convinced that it is so for all numbers.

Some math books answer the question "Why are the above statements true?" by saying that multiplication is "distributive over addition." To most people, this won't be very helpful. In any case, it is not an explanation, just the same fact said in other words.

Perhaps if we see clearly enough that what I have been writing about *is* just a fact of nature, we may not need an explanation. The question "Why is it so?" does not make any more sense than asking why it is that we can split a group of 7 objects into a group of 3 objects and a group of 4 objects. It is so because that's what happens. There isn't some other deeper truth hiding behind that truth.

Well, to return to our fact about multiplying, one way of seeing that it is true, and is always true, and must be true, is by realizing that when we double a recipe we have to double everything in the recipe. If a recipe calls for two eggs, and we want to double it, we have to use four eggs. If it calls for a cup of flour, and we want to double it, we have to add two cups of flour. Even people who are afraid of numbers and arithmetic will see and feel sure that this is true.

And we can see that it is true that if one group of 7 objects can be made into a group of 3 objects and another group of 4 objects, then two groups of 7 objects can be made into two groups of 3 and two groups of 4:

*** ****

*** ****

and that three 7's can be made into three 3's and three 4's:

```
*** ****
*** ****
*** ****
```

and so on.

This is handy for multiplication, because if we didn't know this was so, and wanted to multiply 67 times 8, we would have to write down eight 67's and add them up. But instead of that we say that $67 = 60 + 7$, so all we have to do is multiply 60×8 (which is 480), and 7×8 (which is 56), and then add $480 + 56$, which equals 536. We could write this:

$$67 \times 8 = (60 \times 8) + (7 \times 8)$$
$$= \quad 480 \quad + \quad 56$$
$$= \quad 536$$

From this it is only an easy step or two to the "rule" or trick or procedure or (as mathematicians call it) the "algorithm" for multiplying multiplace numbers (that is, the multiplication we learned in school). I won't go through it here; it is in any arithmetic text.

However, I wouldn't be in too big a hurry to move children from the longer way of doing multiplication, in which they understand all the steps, to the shorter way approved in school. After all, it isn't that much shorter—all it saves us is writing a few extra zeros. This is not worth the confusion we get when we push children too quickly into it.

Thus, if we had 562×74, we might just as well write 562×70 and then 562×4, then figure out those products and add them together to get our final answer. If children get interested in shortcuts, fine, but there is certainly no point in drilling children for weeks or months, as in school, to learn a slightly shorter way to do a calculation that in real life they will rarely have to do.

Fractions

W hen I first taught fifth grade, before I had "taught" the children anything about fractions, or even mentioned the word, I used to ask them questions like this: "If you had three candy bars, and wanted to divide them evenly among five people, how would you do it?" Most of them could think of one or more ways to do this. But after they had "had" fractions, and had learned to think of this as a problem that you had to use fractions to solve, most of them couldn't do it. Instead of reality, and their own common sense and ingenuity, they now had "rules," which they could never keep straight or remember how to apply.

In *What Do I Do Monday?*, I tried to explain how some of this trouble arises:

> As is so often true, our explanations cause more con-
> fusion than they clear up. Most of us, when the time
> comes to "show" and "explain" how to add $\frac{1}{2}$ and $\frac{1}{3}$, say
> that they have to be changed into sixths "because you
> can't add apples and oranges." Something like that. . . .
> The statement is both false in fact and absurd. Of course
> we can add apples and oranges. Every week or two I
> go to the supermarket, put a plastic sack of apples in
> the cart, then go down the counter and drop in a sack
> of oranges. I am adding apples and oranges. In the same
> way, a farmer may put some cows in a barn and then
> later some horses, thus adding horses to cows. Or a
> used-car dealer may drive six Fords onto his lot, and
> follow them with five Chevys, thus adding Chevys to
> Fords.

The trouble is that we haven't said what we meant, because we haven't thought enough about what we meant. What truth are we groping for?

What is really odd is that many children know, or could easily figure out, the answer to this puzzle. I once asked some six-year-olds, "If I put three horses into an empty pasture, and then put two cows in, what would I have in the pasture?" After thinking a while, several of them said, "Five animals."

The first part of the truth we are groping for when we make our confusing statement about apples and oranges is that when we say that we can or cannot add this or that, we are really talking not about the adding itself, but about the way we will express our answer. We can add anything to anything. The real problem is, how shall we talk about the result? The second part of our missing truth is this. It is because we want to find *one number*—hence numerator—to describe the collection of things we have made by adding apples and oranges, or horses and cows, or Chevys and Fords, that we have to find *one name*—hence denominator—to apply to all the objects in our collection. A name is a class, so we have to think about a class to which all the members of the collection belong. Simple enough. This is what the little children saw easily when they said that if I added three horses and two cows, I would have five animals. If I want to apply a single number—numerator—to all the apples and oranges in my basket, I have to think of a class to which they both belong, a name that I can give to all of them, a common name, a common denominator. So I call them fruit. If the used-car dealer, having put several Fords and Chevys on his lot, wants to say what he has there, he can say, "I have five Chevys and six Fords." But if he only wants to use one number to describe his collection, he has to have one name to apply to it, a common denominator. So he says he has eleven automobiles. If he was a dealer in farm machinery, and had in his lot not just cars, but tractors, bulldozers, et cetera, he would have to say, "I have so and so many machines."

Now the case of fractions is only a very special case of this. If I put half a pie on a plate, and then add to it a third of that same pie (or of another pie of the same size), what can I say about what is on my plate? I can say that I have half of a pie and one-third of a pie. Or I can say that I have two *pieces* of pie. In this case, "pieces" is a perfectly good common denominator. What it doesn't tell me, of course, is how much pie I have on my plate, whether the pieces are little or big. So I have to do two things. First, find names, denominators, for my pieces of pie that will tell me how much of the whole pie they are. Secondly, arrange things so that both of my pieces have the same name, a common denominator. I can do this by saying that the big piece is three-sixths of the pie, and the small piece is two-sixths of the pie. It is then easy to see that when we add these two together we can call our result five-sixths of a pie.

Having talked about pies I will now say that it is a mistake to use pies and pie diagrams to introduce children to the idea of fractions, for the very simple reason that there is no way for a child to check, either by inspection or measurement (unles he can measure angles), whether his ideas about adding fractions make any sense or not. Give a child a 6-inch-long strip of paper and a ruler, and ask him to find what half of that piece of paper, plus a third of that same piece, would add up to, and he has a fair chance of coming up with the answer, 5 inches. He can see the reality of what he's doing. This is much less true, or not true at all, of pie diagrams. I remember once carefully making, on cross-ruled (graph) paper, a rectangle nine squares long by three squares wide, and then asking a fifth grader to show me one third of it. Into the middle of this narrow rectangle he put his old familiar one-third pie diagram, then looked at me with great satisfaction. Of course, I tried to tell him that pie diagrams only work for pies, or circles. This obviously seemed to him like one more unnecessarily confusing thing that grown-ups like to tell you. All his other teachers, when *they* wanted to illustrate fractions, drew pie diagrams; therefore, pie diagrams *were* fractions. Of course, in time I was able to persuade him that when he was working with me he had to use some other recipe, some other system, that I happened to like. But his real ideas about fractions, such as they were, did not change.

The last thing in the world I am suggesting is that we should throw at children all these words about cows and fruit and animals and cars, or that if we do, they will all know how to add unlike fractions. I do say that if we, unlike so many arithmetic teachers, know what *we* are doing when we add unlike fractions, and don't talk nonsense about it, we will have a much better chance of finding things to do or say, or materials and projects for the children to work with, that will help them make sense of all this.

On "Infinity"

A mother once wrote me a wonderful letter about her six-year-old's thinking and questions about numbers. One of his questions was "What is the number next to infinity?" I thought about this interesting question and explained, in reply, that there is no number before "infinity." Kids talk about "infinity" as if it were a number, but it isn't. The word *infinite* means "endless" or "boundless." You can't get to the end, or the edge, because there isn't one; no matter how far up you go, you can keep on going. Not an easy idea, maybe, for a six-year-old, or even most adults, to grasp.

The family or, as mathematicians would say, the "class" of whole numbers (that is, 1, 2, 3, 4, 5 ...), *has* no biggest number. No matter how big a number we think of, we can always add some other number to it, or multiply it by another number. Mathematicians call this kind of class of numbers not "infinite" but "transfinite."

There's a good chapter about transfinite numbers in a fascinating book called *Mathematics and the Imagination*, by Kastner and Newman, unfortunately out of print. We learn that one transfinite class, such as the class of even numbers, is the same size as another transfinite class, the class of *all* whole numbers. It seems crazy at first that there can be as many even numbers as there are numbers, since half the numbers are odd. Well, we can say that one class of things is the same size as another class of things if for every item in the first class we can match one and just one item in the second class. If for each right shoe we have one and only one left shoe, then we have just as many right shoes as left shoes, even if we don't know exactly how many we have. For every number in the class of whole numbers 1, 2, 3 ..., we can make one and only one even number, by multiplying the first number times 2. One matches with 2, 2 matches with 4, 3 matches with 6, 4 with 8, 5 with 10, and so on, no matter how far we go. So we can say those two classes are the same size.

There is a wonderful proof, what mathematicians call "elegant" (and it is, too), that the class of fractions is the same size as the class of whole numbers. That really is hard to believe, since between any two whole numbers you can put as many fractions as you want. But there is a way to do that matching game again, so it must be true. There is another elegant proof that the class of decimals is larger than the class of whole numbers.

The mathematician who did a lot of early work on

this, Georg Kantor, showed that some transfinite numbers are bigger than others. Indeed, I think he found four or five different transfinite numbers, each bigger than the one before. The class of whole numbers was the smallest, the class of decimals the next smallest. Then a still larger one, which represented (among other things) a class of all functions.

These are big ideas for a six-year-old (or anyone) to grapple with. If the child asks about infinity, one can try them out and see what happens. If the child turns away and starts to look at something else, enough is enough. In any case, talk about "infinite" instead of "infinity." There is no such *thing*, or mathematical idea, as "infinity." There is just the adjective *infinite*, meaning, as I said before, without an end or an edge.

Bootleg Math

The school I went to for my first four years was very traditional. It taught arithmetic by pure rote memorization, as if we were parrots, or talking laboratory rats. No teacher that I can remember ever discussed mathematical ideas with us, or showed us interesting mathematical tricks. All they did was give us "facts," show us how to do problems, give and correct homework, and drill and test us.

But just as we children had our private secret world of games, so we had our private mathematical world as well. A number of mathematical tricks and games floated round the school, certainly not encouraged by the teachers, and perhaps without their even knowing about them. Often we worked on these mathematical games in class or study hall, hiding our work behind our official math books.

One of these games was "Think of a Number." Student

A would come up to student B, preferably with students C, D, and E nearby, and there would follow a conversation about like this:

A: Think of a number. Don't tell me what it is, but be sure to remember it.

B: OK, I've got it.

A: Make sure you don't forget it!

B: Don't worry, I won't!

A: Now add three to it—and don't tell me the answer.

B: Got it.

A: Now add ten to it.

B: Got it.

A: Now take away seven from it. (*No one ever said "subtract," though the teachers tried to make us.*)

B: OK.

A: Now add five to it.

B: OK.

A: Now take away the number you started with.

B: OK.

A: (Triumphantly) The answer is eleven!

At this point B, C, and D would challenge A to do the trick again. It might take A several times to convince them that he really knew how to do the trick, and could do it as many times as he wanted. At which point they would walk away, shaking their heads and wondering. Or maybe they would beg him to show them how to do the trick.

No child I knew ever showed another child how to do this trick. Yet every year a gang of us would figure it out and learn to do it, while a new bunch of recruits would come into the school, ready to be tricked and mystified in their turn.

As far as I remember, none of us who did the trick

ever wrote down all the operations we asked the others to do. We would do them all in our heads, a step at a time. The longer we could keep going, the more baffled the others would be when we came up with the right answer.

Once in a while someone, perhaps the trickster, although usually his subject, would make a mistake in adding or subtracting, and the final answers would not agree. A heated and noisy argument would follow, which was usually settled by the trickster demanding a chance to do the trick again. If the answers disagreed two or more times, the trickster would insist that the subject couldn't add properly, and would look for someone else to work on. Since subjects were usually younger than tricksters, we generally accepted this view of the matter.

I would guess that children just beginning to add would find this trick quite exciting.

Another math game that my friends and I used to play in school—a game that the teachers had nothing to do with and may not even have known about—had to be done on paper. Since it took some time, we had to be careful not to get caught doing it.

We would begin with a piece of paper ruled into squares. Since we didn't have graph paper, we had to measure and rule these squares ourselves. Usually a grid of 10×10 squares was big enough for us, though sometimes, for more elaborate shapes, we would make a bigger one.

Then on our grid we would make a shape, by drawing straight lines from one grid intersection to another, and so on around until our shape was completed. The shape might be a simplified dog, or sailboat, or airplane, or simply a shape. For the "dog," we would begin (with the dog's nose) somewhere near the left edge of the grid. Then we would say, "Go up two squares and two squares over to the right." That would give us our second point. Then we'd say, "Go down two squares and two squares over to the right." That would give our third point. Then, "Four squares over to the right," and so on until the "dog" was finished:

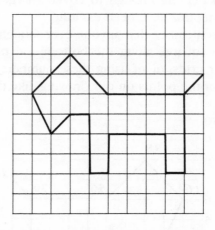

Then came the exciting part of the game. Again we would draw a 10 × 10 grid, but this time with the squares much bigger or smaller than the first one. On this new grid we would make a shape, following exactly the same steps we had taken to make our first shape, beginning with our starting point, then going up two squares and two over to the right, and so on until the shape was completed. Then we would compare this new drawing with our first drawing. We were always absolutely astonished to find that our new shape looked exactly like the first one, only a different size. It seemed like a miracle. We did it over and over again, and every time were just as surprised and delighted to find that our second shape was just like our first one, only smaller, or bigger.

Since we were "spozed" to be working on regular arithmetic, and we had to keep our pictures hidden, we couldn't get a great variation in size. But if the teachers had known about this game, and had wanted to encourage it, we might have been able to copy a shape from little teeny squares to great big ones, even on a sheet of paper big enough to cover a large part of a wall. That *would* have been exciting.

I don't remember that anyone ever thought of numbering the squares along the bottom and up the left side of our grids, or of using these numbers to locate each one of the points on our drawing, like this:

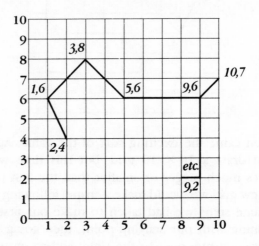

The idea that you could make a shape and then tell someone else how to make a shape just like yours by giving him nothing but a bunch of numbers would have been exciting for us. It would have seemed another miracle.

It would also have led easily into the idea of scale drawings, in which a certain distance on the drawing stands for a certain distance in real life: 1 inch = 1 foot, or 1 inch = 100 miles. From there we might have gone into architectural plans—I have always thought that many children, once they understood what a plan was, would be interested in the project of making a plan of their own room, or house. Our game would also have led us into the basic idea of analytic geometry, graphs of equations, and other interesting ideas that students don't usually meet until late in high school—too late, when all but a few of them have learned to hate and fear math.

Family Economics

Chris, five, enjoys the ancient adding machine in our office. It is a real old-fashioned electromechanical machine, with wheels and gears that go round inside and make interesting noises, and small metal bars that pop up out of the machine in order to print numbers on the paper—really a much more interesting machine for children than an electronic calculator, which works silently, as if by magic. What he likes to do with the machine is punch in a series of numbers, press the button to add them up, tear off the little strip of paper on which the numbers and the total are written, and call that a "check," showing it to one of us and demanding that we cash it, or telling us that he is going to the bank to cash it. I say to him, "Chris, if the bank does cash that piece of paper, be sure to let me know right away, and I'll be down there in one minute." One day he made these same strips of paper and called them a "bill," which he presented to one of us, demanding that we pay it in return for some piece of work he had done.

Again, and as always with children, we see a nice mix of fantasy and reality. I am fairly sure that in sober moments he knows that these scraps of paper are not in fact checks or bills, but he has seen us at work long enough to sense that they do have something to do with the real checks and bills that come into the office, and that these have a lot to do with money.

The first school I taught in had an institution called the Student Bank, run by the school business manager. It was a kind of petty-cash fund for students, and was probably set up because of the fear that if students had much cash around their rooms (it was a boarding school) there might be problems of stealing.

At the beginning of the school year the parents of each student would make a "deposit" in the student's account in the Student Bank (the amount was, in fact, just added to the parents' bill). When students wanted some cash, or wanted to buy books or supplies from the school, they would write out a fake "check" and give it to the business manager, who would then give them the cash, supplies, athletic equipment, or whatever. The manager kept a separate account for each student, just like a real bank, and was also supposed to see that students kept their "checkbooks" balanced. The idea was to give the students some practice in keeping track of their own money and in finding out how banks worked.

During one year I also worked as business manager and had to run the Student Bank. It damn near drove me crazy. Here we were, a few hundred yards from town, *where there was a real bank*. Why not have the students open up accounts in the real bank, write real checks, and get real statements, instead of wasting a lot of my (or someone's) time running a pretend bank?

Obviously in some families the children have so little money that no nearby bank will let them have an account. There is nothing to be done about that. But I feel quite strongly that any children who have enough money so that a local bank will give them an account ought to have one. It is real, grown-up, and interesting— part of the real world out there.

Not many families, however, seem comfortable making children a part of their own financial world. When I was growing up, one of the things my father used to say with real conviction was "The most important thing in the world is the business of earning a living." Except for that, money was never mentioned in front of me and my sisters. I didn't know then, and don't know to this day, how much my father earned, or what other income he may have had, or what taxes we paid, or what rent, or how much my schooling cost, or what our medical bills were, or insurance, or anything. I don't remember that I was particularly curious about these matters, but even if I had been, I would never have dared to ask about them.

I now feel strongly that children should know, or be able to know, the facts about their families' finances— how much money there is, how it is earned or otherwise received, and how it is spent or saved. Children are interested in these things. Money is one of the most mysterious and attractive parts of the adult world they live in and want to find out about. It is obviously important—the grown-ups talk about it all the time.

For another thing, the family finances, the economics of the family, are a small and simple version of the economics of the town, state, country, or world. The more you understand about the economics of your own family, the more you are likely to understand about the economics of larger places.

Also, family economics is a way of talking about numbers and arithmetic in a real context. Instead of learning to use numbers in the abstract, in a kind of vacuum, so that later (at least in theory) they can begin to use them to think about something real, children can begin to think and talk right now about what is real, and as they do it learn to use numbers. Family economics will bring in such ideas as interest, percentage, loans, mortgages, installments, insurance, and so on, that children learning math only in school would not meet for years. And in talking about money we can use different kinds of graphs—bar graphs or circle graphs to show how income and expenses are divided up, or graphs of various quantities against time, to show how various expenses vary through the year (more heat in winter), or from year to year.

Families with little money often find it hard to explain to their children why they don't have or can't have something they want. A father wrote me that he was having a terrible time convincing his child that at the moment he couldn't get him a ten-speed bike. I suggested that he show him exactly how much money the family earned, what it had to spend money on, and what it had to save money for, and let the child see for himself that the bicycle money wasn't there. He said he would. How this worked out, he never told me. At any rate, the child may have learned something worth knowing.

As with everything else, some children will be much more interested in these money matters than others. If children are not interested, let it go, and just keep the information where they can get it if they want to. But some other children may even want, at least for a while, to keep the family books, records of all the money that comes in and goes out. Here again, I wouldn't turn such a project into a compulsory chore. Some quite young children might well start such a project, only to lose interest in it after a while. Let them drop it. Others would be willing and even eager to do the project over a long period of time. In that case, offer them even more responsibility. Let them write checks and pay bills, balance the checkbook, and so on.

Solving Problems

A mong the large and important questions about math is the question that millions of tormented schoolchildren must have asked themselves over the years: "What is math *for*, anyway?"

The answer, as I eventually figured out for myself, long after I was out of school, is that people invented math partly for the reason that they invented music— it was fascinating and beautiful—and partly for the practical reason that it helped them solve problems that they wanted or needed to solve and could not solve, or solve as easily, any other way. One of the earliest of these may have been "How can I be sure that all the sheep I went out with in the morning are with me when I bring them home at night?" Another might have been "How can I tell how big my field is if every spring the floods of the Nile wipe out all of the boundary marks?"

It is exciting to figure out how to solve a problem that you really want to solve. Yet, when I talk to meetings of teachers about children and learning, it often happens that someone says, usually in an angry tone of voice, "Learning can't be all fun!" (What they usually mean by this is "Learning can't *ever* be fun, or it isn't really learning.") They are so wrong about this. Figuring things out, solving problems, is about as much fun as anything we human beings know how to do. For pleasure and excitement, hardly anything beats it, and few things even come close.

The strategy of solving problems is called "heuristics":

in other words, what you do when you are not sure what to do. Take a common problem like figuring out percentages. Many people are never sure which number to divide into which. One way to figure this out is to start with a very simple problem, one to which you know the answer, and try out various possible methods on that problem. Assuming that you know that 50 percent of something means half of it, make up a very simple problem, of which you know that 50 percent will be the right answer. Thus: "There are six people in a room, and three of them are women. What percentage of the people in the room are women?" You have a 3 and a 6 there, and are not sure which to divide into which. If you divide the 3 into the 6, you get the answer 2, and no matter what you do with the decimal point, you can't make that turn into a 50. So you divide the 6 into the 3 and get .5 for an answer. Well, .5 is not 50, but you can make it 50 by moving the decimal two places to the right. So it looks as if, to find what percentage a small thing is of a big thing, you divide the big thing into the small thing, and then multiply your answer by 100 (or move your decimal point two places to the right, which is the same thing as multiplying by 100).

Or, you could say to yourself, "1 is 50 percent of 2," which would suggest that you had to divide the 2 into the 1, rather than the other way around.

Or, you might say to yourself, "Since 50 percent is the same as $\frac{1}{2}$, then 50 percent must mean the same as $\frac{50}{100}$ or fifty one-hundredths."

In other words, start with what you know, and use a little guesswork, or common sense, or whatever you want to call it, to figure out what you don't know.

When I was in school, scientists and engineers used slide rules to do quick calculations. I knew that slide rules existed, but had never used one. One day I found myself in a spot where, in a short time, I had to do a lot of problems involving calculation. I knew that the only way I could get them done was by using a slide rule, but obviously I had to first figure out how. So I made up some very simple problems, like $2 \times 3 = 6$, and then pushed and pulled things around on the slide rule until I got the right answer. Then I checked that with a couple of other simple problems, and when the method worked with them, I knew I could use the slide rule on the harder problems. When you're not sure which of two or three methods to use, then try all of them on a simple problem and see which one gives you the answer that you know is right.

The pleasure of solving a problem does not always come all at one sitting, or from one day to the next as in homework problems. I once worked on a problem for over twenty years. The problem had to do with a family of numbers called "factorials." Quite a long time ago, mathematicians became interested in this family of numbers:

$$1$$
$$1 \times 2$$
$$1 \times 2 \times 3$$
$$1 \times 2 \times 3 \times 4$$
$$1 \times 2 \times 3 \times 4 \times 5, \text{ et cetera}$$

Someone invented a name and a symbol for these numbers, calling 1×2 "2 factorial," and $1 \times 2 \times 3$ "3 factorial," and writing them "2!," "3!," and so on.

When people think about numbers and their properties, the kinds of things we can or can't do with them, one of the elementary properties they look into is what can these numbers be divided by.

One of the things they soon saw about factorials was that:

4! could *not* be divided by 5
5! *could* be divided by 6
6! could *not* be divided by 7
7! *could* be divided by 8
8! *could* be divided by 9
9! *could* be divided by 10
10! could *not* be divided by 11
11! divisible by 12 Yes
12! divisible by 13 No
13! divisible by 14 Yes

It became obvious that a factorial could not be divided by the next higher number if that next number was what they call "prime," which means that it can be divided evenly only by itself and 1. (The prime numbers are 2, 3, 5, 7, 11, 13, 17, 19, 23, 29, 31, 37, 41, 43, 47, 53, 59, et cetera. Some mathematicians, as I said, are still trying to find a formula for *all* prime numbers.)

With a little more looking they saw this pattern:

4! + 1 is divisible by 5
6! + 1 is divisible by 7
10! + 1 is divisible by 11
12! + 1 is divisible by 13

and so on.

When mathematicians find something like this, that seems to be true for many numbers, they begin to ask themselves whether it is true for all numbers, and whether they can prove that it is. If and when they can, they have what they call a theorem. The particular theorem about factorials, which challenged me for so long, was written like this:

Where N is any prime number,
(N − 1)! + 1 is divisible by N

By modern standards, this is very primitive math. I don't know when this particular theorem was proved, or by whom—it may go back to the classical Greeks. In any case, finding the proof was an exciting adventure for me.

I ran across this theorem in a book called, I think, *The World of Numbers*. At one point the author gave two theorems about factorials, saying that although the proof of these theorems did not involve anything more than simple algebra, probably only people with quite a bit of mathematical talent would be able to work them out. Thus challenged, I began to work on the first theorem (I have long since forgotten the second). I spent hours on it, and got nowhere. I decided that I was going to work it out, no matter how long it took.

I never read any farther in the book, because I feared that I might see the proof somewhere, and so would never be able to find it for myself. I worked on the problem again a few days later. Again, nothing. And I continued to work on it since. Sometimes I forgot it for as long as a year or more; then something has reminded me of it and I have tried again, always without success.

Once, a few years ago, I thought I had a proof—but realized after a while that I had done some circular reasoning, and that my proof was no good.

About two days ago something put it in my mind, and I began to work on it again. I tried a new, or almost new, approach. It looked interesting, but after a while it had not led me anywhere. The work had made me sleepy, so I lay down for a short nap. I woke thinking of the problem, seeing some of the symbols in my mind. Still half-asleep, I tried a couple of steps. They led to something I couldn't remember having done before. I considered it for a second, then sat up, wide awake, saying, "It can't be that easy." I grabbed some paper and wrote out the steps I had done in my half-awake mind. They were OK. I hadn't made any mistakes. Would my proof work for all cases? Yes, it would. I could hardly believe it—it was so easy, only five steps. I realized that I had been close to it all those years. How could I have missed it? Anyway, now I had it. A fine feeling.

Riding, Hunting, and Arithmetic

Alison Stallibrass, author of *The Self-Respecting Child*, recently sent me a lovely passage by the British essayist William Cobbett from his book *Rural Rides* (1825). He was one of the true characters of English literature, first of all a countryman and farmer, but also a journalist and pamphleteer, a fearless and determined opponent of corruption and a defender of political liberty in the late eighteenth and early nineteenth centuries, when liberty was a risky thing to defend. At one point he was jailed for his writings, and while he was in jail, his children, none of them older than sixteen or so, ran his large farm very competently, keeping him fully informed about its doing in the letters they sent him along with baskets of food.

Cobbett was a wonderfully opinionated and outspoken man. Two things above all others could rouse him to passion. One was potatoes, which were then coming very much into fashion and which he felt were a terrible crop. The other was Shakespeare. People who had an overdose of Shakespeare in their schooling will get much pleasure out of what Cobbett had to say about him.

Here is some of what Cobbett wrote about education, and arithmetic in particular, that illustrates much of what I have been trying to say in this chapter and elsewhere:

Richard [his son] and I have done something else be-sides ride, and hunt, and course, and stare about us, during this last month. He was eleven years old last March, and it was now time for him to begin to know something about letters and figures. He has learned to work in the garden, and having been a good deal in the country, knows a great deal about farming affairs. . . . When he and I went from home, I had business in Reigate. It was a very wet morning, and we went off long before daylight in a post chaise, intending to have our horses brought after us.

. . . He had learned from mere play to read, being first set to work of his own accord to find out what was said about Thurtell, when all the world was talking and reading about Thurtell. That had induced us to give him *Robinson Crusoe*; and that had made him a passable reader. Then he had scrawled down letters and words upon paper, and had written letters to me in the strang-est way imaginable. His knowledge of figures he had acquired from the necessity of knowing the several numbers upon the barrels of seeds brought from Amer-ica, and the numbers upon the doors of houses.

. . . I began with a pretty long lecture on the utility of arithmetic; the absolute necessity of it, in order for us to make out our accounts of the trees and seeds that we should have to sell in the winter, and the utter impossibility of our getting paid for our pains unless we were able to make out our accounts. . . . Having thus made him understand the utility of the thing, and given him a very strong instance of the case of our nursery affairs, I proceeded to explain to him the meaning of the word arithmetic, the power of figures, according to the place they occupied. I then, for it was still dark, taught him to add a few figures together, I naming the figures one after another, while he, at the mention of each new figure said the amount, and if incorrectly, he was corrected by me. When we had got a sum of about 24, I said now there is another line of figures on the left of this, and therefore you are to put down the 4 and carry the 2. "What is carrying?" said he. I then explained to him the why and the wherefore of this, and he perfectly understood me at once. We then did several other little sums; and by the time we got to Sutton, it became daylight, I took up a pencil and set him a little sum upon paper, which, after making a mistake or two, he did very well.

By the time we got to Reigate he had done several more, and at last a pretty long one, with very few errors. We had business all day, and thought no more of our scholarship until we went to bed, and then we did, in our post-chaise fashion, a great many lines in arithmetic before we went to sleep. Thus we went on mixing our riding and hunting with our arithmetic, until we quitted Godalming, when he did a sum very nicely in multiplication of money, falling a little short of what I had laid out, which was to make him learn the four rules in whole numbers first, and then in money, before I got home.

... Now when there is so much talk about education, let me ask how many pounds it generally costs parents to have a boy taught this much of arithmetic; how much time it costs also; and, which is a far more serious consideration, how much mortification, and very often how much loss of health, it costs the poor scolded broken-hearted child, who becomes dunder-headed and dull for all this life-time, merely because that has been imposed upon him as a task which he ought to regard as an object of pleasant pursuit. I never even once desired him to stay a moment from any other thing that he had a mind to go at. I just wrote the sums down upon paper, laid them upon the table, and left him to tackle them when he pleased.

In the case of the multiplication table, the learning of which is something of a job, and which it is absolutely necessary to learn perfectly, I advised him to go up into his bedroom and read it twenty times over out loud every morning before he went a hunting, and ten times over every night after he came back, till it all came as pat upon his lips as the names of persons that he knew. He did this, and at the end of about a week he was ready to set upon multiplication. It is the irksomeness of the thing which is the greatest bar to learning of every sort. I took care not to suffer irksomeness to seize his mind for a moment, and the consequence was that which I have described. . . .

. . . I look upon my boy as being like other boys in general. Their fathers can teach arithmetic as well as I; and if they have not a mind to pursue my method, they must pursue their own. Let them apply to the outside of the head and to the back, if they like; let them bargain for thumps and the birch rod; it is their affair and not mine. I never yet saw in my house a child that was *afraid*, that was in any fear whatever; that was ever for a moment under any sort of apprehension, on account of the learning of anything; and I never in my life gave a command, an order, a request, or even advice, to look in any book; and I am quite satisfied that the way to make children dunces, to make them detest books, and justify the detestation, is to tease them and bother them upon the subject.

As to age at which children ought to begin to be taught, it is very curious that, while I was at a friend's house during my ride, I looked into, by mere accident, a little child's abridgement of the History of England. . . . The historian had introduced the circumstance of Alfred's father, who, "through a *mistaken notion* of kindness to his son, had suffered him to live to the age of twelve years without any attempt being made to give him education." How came this writer to know that it was a *mistaken notion*? Ought he not rather, when he looked at the result, when he considered the astonishing knowledge and great deeds of Alfred, ought he not to have hesitated before he thus criticized the notions of the father? . . . I am satisfied that if they had begun to thump the head of Alfred when he was a child, we should not at this day hear talk of Alfred the Great.

Young Children as Research Scientists

The process by which children
turn experience into knowledge is
exactly the same, point for point,
as the process by which those
whom we call scientists make
scientific knowledge.

Puzzles

One Sunday morning as I was walking up Boylston Street I saw a young mother waiting in a restaurant lobby, watching as her fifteen-month-old baby boy explored the place. She was wonderful with him and gave him lots of room. She didn't try to show him things, or help him unless he asked for help. This being one of my favorite forms of entertainment, I stopped and watched him for quite a while. The baby had a couple of colored plastic rings, which he was using as bracelets. He would put them on one of his arms, then later take them off. Quite often he would put them both on his arm at the same time, which he had no trouble with. But sometimes the two would get separated. He would put one bracelet on his arm, up by the elbow. Then he appeared to think to himself, "Now, this other bracelet ought to be right alongside it." But what he would do then would be to put the free bracelet, so to speak, *against* the part of his arm where the other bracelet was, as if some kind of attraction would hold it there. He had in mind the image of the two bracelets on his arm, and wanted to make that happen again. But once he had one bracelet on his arm, he could only think of somehow putting the other bracelet next to it; he couldn't remember *how* that first bracelet had got on his arm, or do the same thing with the second bracelet. He could put both on together, but he couldn't put on first one and then the other. I found myself wondering at what point he would solve his puzzle. As nice as the mother was, I think it's possible that she may not have noticed this little puzzle that her tiny boy was trying unsuccessfully to solve. On the other hand, perhaps she did. But it is from a great many minute and close observations of this kind that we learn something about children and their learning, and how we may help (or impede) that learning.

Children are born passionately eager to make as much sense as they can of things around them. The process by which children turn experience into knowledge is exactly the same, point for point, as the process by which those whom we call scientists make scientific knowledge. Children observe, they wonder, they speculate, and they ask themselves questions. They think up possible answers, they make theories, they hypothesize, and then they test theories by asking questions or by further observations or experiments or reading. Then they modify the theories as needed, or reject them, and the process continues. This is what in "grown-up" life is called the—capital *S*, capital *M*—Scientific Method. It is precisely what these little guys start doing as soon as they are born.

If we attempt to control, manipulate, or divert this process, we disturb it. If we continue this long enough, the process stops. The independent scientist in the child disappears.

Creating Knowledge

The mother of J. P., four years old, wrote me a delightful letter describing how her son goes about building his mental model of the world:

He wants to know about death, and where babies come from, and whether I still love him when I'm mad at him—and those are the *easy* questions! Some of the stuff he comes up with is really startling, like "If there was a hole under our house, why wouldn't it fall all the way to the other side of the world?" and "Why can't you make a car that runs on hydrogen?" (He *must* have heard somebody talking about that sometime, but the way it came up, we had been looking up what makes balloons rise, and he had asked what makes cars go, a few days before.) Sometimes the questions he asks sound strange, because he's thinking about things he doesn't have the words for yet, like the other day: "How do cats know to be a cat, when they just eat and aren't there?" I *think* that means, "How is a specific body form created and maintained without an intelligence-in-residence directing the process?" I had a craven impulse just to say, "God does it," but instead I told him I didn't know—let him read about theology vs. evolution for himself.

J. P. is very interested in gardening and living things. Did you know that if you take a few scale divisions off a lily bulb before you plant it, and put them in a plastic bag with a little semi-moist peat moss, they'll make tiny new lily bulbs, right in your kitchen? J. P. was fascinated with mine, so we made him a "nursery pot" of his own, with his very own "lily-babies" in it (once they were big enough to leave their "mommies"). I gave him all the ones that grew a leaf, and to make it more interesting, I cut some pictures out of an old catalog of the flowers they'll have and stapled them on plastic markers, to put next to each bulb. J. P. mixes up "secret formula" fertilizers for them out of mud, bone meal, eggshells, rock phosphate, and whatever else he can scrounge in the greenhouse, and feeds it to them with a turkey baster (I just have to keep him from drowning them). The very first word that J. P. ever spelled on his own was "lily." He wrote it out on an extra seed catalog order form I'd given him. I wasn't paying much attention when he told me he was sending for some lily-babies, but there it was, clear as anything.

Here we have a wonderful picture of a four-year-old human being doing what all human beings of that age, and other ages, do (though no two of them do it the same way): exploring the world around him, *creating* knowledge out of his own questions, thoughts, and experiences. All children do this, as we see when we pay a little thoughtful attention to them.

Building Understanding

As children go about trying to explore and understand the world, many of the adults to whom they turn with questions are not as helpful as J. P.'s mother. It is useful not only for the children in our lives, but for our own learning, to think about what understanding, or the lack of it, actually means.

When we don't understand something, one or more of three things are happening. First of all, we may have heard a word or words, or seen a sign, for which we don't know the *referent* (which means the object, thing, or experience that the word or sign refers to). Thus, the referent of the word *dog* is a four-legged furry animal, usually with a tail. If you had never seen a dog, and someone mentioned the name in conversation, you'd be a little puzzled. Or if you were an Eskimo, and someone mentioned a giraffe (I can't imagine why), again, you'd be puzzled. If you had lived only in the far North, it would be very hard to "explain" to you what a tree was. Or a mountain, if you lived on flat tundra. People who have never seen snow, even though they have heard of it and even seen photos of it, are usually bowled over when they see the real thing.

If you had seen *some* animals—say, a horse or a cat—
I could explain a dog pretty easily, could say that it was
smaller than a horse but about the same size as or bigger
than a cat, with four legs, a head, and a tail. If you had
never seen a four-legged animal at all, it might be a little
bit hard to explain how a four-legged animal is put
together. You could perhaps draw a picture. But people
who have no experience of pictures, primitive tribes,
cannot connect in their minds pictures of things with
the real things, cannot even recognize a picture of themselves or their own house.

Another hurdle to understanding is to hear one thing
and then another that seems to contradict the first. If
you had been told that ducks fly in the air, and that
snapping turtles live in the water, and later heard someone say that a duck had been caught by a snapping
turtle (which happens), you would be confused. How
could that be possible? Someone would then have to
say that ducks also live some of the time in water, at
which point you would understand.

A third problem in understanding is difficulty in making a connection. When someone tells us one thing that
seems to make sense, and then some other thing that
also seems to make sense, sometimes we can't see how
they are connected, what they have to do with each
other. If someone tells us something that we think we
understand, but it doesn't seem to connect with anything, we think, "Why are you telling me that?"

Knowing how understanding works can be useful for
anyone trying to learn or to explain something to someone else. If you find, reading or hearing someone else
talk, that you don't understand something, don't panic.
Take a few minutes to ask yourself which of those three
cases you are in. If you are reading, and are not sure
what the referent of a word or phrase is, what thing is
being described, you can ask someone, or look it up in

a dictionary, or, if the book is a textbook, look it up in the index at the back of the book, see on which page the word first appears, and then see what it says about the word on that page.

If your problem is that two things seem to contradict each other, it will help to say as accurately as you can what the contradiction is, thus: "It says that ducks fly in the air, and that snapping turtles live in the water, so how could a snapping turtle catch a duck?" That is an easy question for someone else to answer.

When a student says to a teacher, "I don't get it," there isn't much the teacher can do about it. If children seem puzzled, ask them to describe the object or situation as they see it, so that the source of confusion will eventually surface. The more precisely we say what it is that confuses us, the easier it will be for someone else to help clear up the confusion.

Making Our Own Connections

Jacob Bronowski, in *Science and Human Values*, made the point, very beautifully and graphically, that to discover the connection between what had seemed two isolated facets of existence is a creative act, whether the field is art or science. He calls it an act of unifying. This is something we cannot do for someone else. We cannot make these connections in someone else's mind. We can give them data. We can even tell them what the connection is. But we must not assume because we have told them, and because they can repeat what we have said, that they really know. They have to discover this for themselves.

That is not to say that children must discover everything unaided. We can help them in several ways. We can so arrange the materials put before them that discovery is made more likely. Real learning is a process of discovery, and if we want it to happen, we must create the kinds of conditions in which discoveries are made. We know what these are. They include time, leisure, freedom, and lack of pressure.

In high school I studied physics, and soon ran into Newton's third law of motion. My reaction to it was to say that it was poppycock. I had been thinking about the problem for years. At the age of about ten or eleven I had had an argument with some aunts and uncles about rocket ships in space, and I had argued very convincingly that a rocket would not work in space, because there was nothing, no air, for the gas to push against. How can you push when there is nothing to push against? I was so convincing that to this day I cannot persuade them that I was on the wrong side of the argument. In high school I was told that when I pushed against a wall the wall pushed back. What non-sense! One minute the wall is standing there, not push-ing; the next minute it is pushing. How does it decide to make the change? And as for the notion that the earth turns slightly under your feet when you walk on it— moonshine! It took a long time to discover for myself that the third law was true. Nobody did it for me; nobody could have done it for me. And, of course, all the time I was grappling with the problem I was handing in physics papers saying things that I did not believe. Eventually I felt in my bones the truth of what Newton was talking about, so much so that now, when running, I really do feel my feet turning the earth under me.

But what often happens to kids in school is that they are required to repeat, as sense, what makes no sense to them, to the point where they give up trying to reconcile what people say about the world with what they really feel about it. They accept as true whatever authority says is true. They do not try to check or test it. They soon forget even how to test it. Oh, sure, it is easy to test the statement that water boils at such and such a temperature; but most of our knowledge, most of what we are asked to accept as true, cannot be so easily tested. I cannot run controlled experiments to test the truth of what people tell me about history, or economics, or human nature. I have to check these statements against my mental model, such as it is.

Lessons in the Field

Recently a young friend with an interest in home schooling was invited by a wealthy family on a tropical island to tutor their son for a year or two. At the time, my friend was on the staff of the New Alchemy Institute, an environmental organization devoted to the development of sustainable agriculture and appropriate technology. He wrote me to ask how to plan the boy's "curriculum." I answered him as follows:

> Since the young person lives in one of the most unusual biological places in the world, it would be foolish not to make that habitat and its special life forms a central part of your study. You should make it an important part of *your* business to learn as much as you can about this place, and have him learn with you.
>
> I think it would be a very good idea to write this boy a letter, quite a long one, telling him something about yourself, your work, your interests, and your particular interests in the islands, and ask him to write you back telling you something about himself and his life and interests. . . . The point is that you have as much to learn about this boy's world as he has to learn about yours. In teaching you, he will learn a great deal about himself.
>
> You should tell this boy something of the work of the New Alchemists. Part of your work should be consid-

ering what a New Alchemist project on the islands might do. From their location I would guess that they are very windy, and also, that they have to pay a lot for electricity. Maybe you could do a study of wind power.

Given your interest in worms, and by extension, other critters that feed on wastes, you might make an inventory of local creatures that could perform such a function.

The thread that is running all through these suggestions of mine is that this boy will learn best and most if his learning grows out of being associated with you in *serious adult work*, not school stuff. In all of these projects that I have suggested there is plenty of mathematics, physics, et cetera. But it will be better if it is rooted in some kind of serious reality.

Since I did not know of books on the particular ecology he would encounter, I left that search up to him. Instead, I suggested that he himself record his experiences, and that the boy he was "tutoring" could join him in writing about their work together.

Putting Meaning into the World

Children do not move from ignorance about a given thing to knowledge of it in one sudden step, like going to a light that has been off and turning it on. For children do not *acquire* knowledge, but *make* it. As I said before, they create knowledge, as scientists do, by observing, wondering, theorizing, and then testing and revising these theories. To go from the point of making a new theory to the point of being sure that it is true often takes them a long time. Usually, children are not aware of these processes, this scientific method that they are continually using; they do not know that they are observing, theorizing, and testing and revising theories, and would be surprised and baffled if you told them so. At any particular moment in their growth their minds are full of theories about various aspects of the world around them, including language, which they are constantly testing, but not for the life of them could they tell you what these theories are. We cannot help these unconscious processes by meddling with them. Even when we are trying our best to be helpful, by assisting or improving these processes, we can only do harm.

Because Jean Piaget, brilliant and original thinker though he was, did not understand this about children, both the method he used to try to learn about children's thinking and the conclusions he drew from it were wrong. Psychologists are increasingly finding in experiments with children that when they give them a way of showing what they know in *actions* instead of words, the results of Piaget's experiments are reversed, and the children show that they are indeed capable of doing many things that he said they could not do. Children as young as two have now been shown to be able to do exactly the kind of formal, logical reasoning that he declared was impossible.

If we want children to do formal reasoning with different kinds of abstract quantities and shapes, whether these be Cuisenaire rods or Montessori materials or lumps of clay, we must give them time to do what I can only call "de-abstracting" these objects: in other words, using fantasy and play to put some real life and meaning into them. Thus, to invent an example, if we give a child a small set of wooden colored blocks to play with, and give her time to invent a game in which these become, say, a Mommy, Daddy, and three children, we cannot then fool that child into saying there are more or fewer blocks just by changing their arrangement in space. Shuffle those blocks around however we will, the child will still recognize that here is the Mommy block, here is the Daddy block, and so on, until all the block family is accounted for.

I think here of E. F. Schumacher's lovely story about the old shepherd. "Don't count the sheep," he said, "or else they won't thrive." By this he meant that if you counted the sheep you would turn each real, live, unique animal into an abstraction or a symbol of a sheep, every one like every other, sheep = sheep = sheep, and so would begin to lose sight of them as individual sheep, and fail to notice whether they were remaining healthy and energetic, their best sheep selves.

What we easily forget, in our passionate twentieth-century love affair with abstract thinking, is that to make an abstraction out of some part of reality we must take some meaning *out* of it. This makes it so much easier for us to think about whatever it is, manipulate it, measure it, put it into numbers, put it into a computer, that we tend more often than not to think that our abstraction is larger and more real than the reality of which it is only a small part, and to ignore the reality we threw away in order to make our abstraction. We think that whatever we can't count, doesn't count. For instance, schools count the children, or countable things they try to get the children to do, and so, like the bad shepherd, they come to think that these numbers are more real than the children themselves. Soon they forget to look at the children, forget even *how* to look at the children. Children resist this continual abstracting because their chief business in life is finding and making meaning, putting meaning *into* a world that must at first seem wholly meaningless to them. It is not a weakness on their part but a strength. They are more passionately interested in reality and meaning than we are, and struggle to preserve it, find it, and invent it, wherever and however they can.

A child of four recently showed me, once again, that little children can and do make use of formal reasoning in their life and growth. Bridget, who often comes to the office with her mother and two sisters, was saying things like "Him moved the boxes" and "Her took the crayons." This surprised me. I have often heard little children say, "Me want this," though not all do—one of my now grown-up niece's first utterances was "I some," meaning "I want some, give me some." But I hadn't heard a child say, "Her do this" or "Him do that." What we have to realize about this is that it is *not* imitation. Bridget has never heard *anyone* use "her" or "him" as the subjects of verbs. This is her own application of her own mini-theory of the English language. In this she is using both inductive and deductive reasoning. From other people's use of the words *her* and *him* she arrived at the correct generalization that these were what we (but not she) call pronouns, words that can stand in the place of a noun or a proper name. From there she deduced her particular rule that she could use these same pronouns as the subjects of verbs. And even as I write about this it occurs to me that she has already stopped doing it—I can't remember her saying that the last few times she has been in the office. So she has already tested her theory about English against her observations of other people's use of it and, seeing that her theory doesn't fit, has changed it. If this is not formal reasoning, nothing is.

Loving Music

I do not think I have ever heard
the voice of God. But I have
certainly heard the voice of Satan.
Sometimes, when I am listening to
beautiful music, that voice
whispers in my ear, "But all it
does is go up and down."

—Unpublished proverbs of
John Holt

Another Chance

Every so often I have a fantasy, a sort of science-fiction fantasy. In this fantasy, some intergalactic federation begins to take note of the fact that the planet Earth, of a particular solar system over at one edge of the Milky Way, is beginning to spew a certain amount of material out into space. The federation decides that it had better go down there and see what these guys are up to. So they send down some representatives to live on earth for a while in disguise and scout around and report back what is going on out there.

After seeing our wars and suffering and nuclear weapons and hydrogen bombs and one thing and another, the scouts get their report together pretty quickly. Basically, they say that these Earth folks are a pretty hard lot, and they recommend wiping them out before they make any more trouble than they already are making. But just before the scouts return with their report, somebody persuades them to go to a concert, or a few concerts, and they hear a chorus, an orchestra, perhaps a cantata, perhaps a string quartet, perhaps . . . , and after they hear it, they think, Well, maybe we'll give these folks another chance.

Starting Early

If you don't start early, it's too late. This is one of the great mythologies of music, a piece of musical folklore. Just as an absolute matter of fact, it is not so.

I would love to have somebody do some serious and extensive research in this area. I would love to do it myself, for that matter, but I have and expect I will have too many other kinds of commitments. But even my rather occasional and informal investigations have turned up much evidence that this piece of folklore is only that. Thus, not long ago I was speaking to a local woman, a professional musician and the manager of a professional-class civic orchestra. She told me that when she went to the Yale School of Music, presumably at age twenty-one or so, she went only as a pianist. As part of her work there she was required to study a second instrument, and took up the viola. Before she left the music school, she was playing at a high enough level to play in the New Haven Symphony, which is a thoroughly professional orchestra. In our conversation she told me that she knows a number of people who play professionally, and I mean not just picking up a little money here and there, but at a high level of skill, who did not begin until their twenties. I have absolutely no reason to doubt that this is so.

There is nothing in logic that supports the idea that it is possible as an adult to *be* skillful enough to play instruments at a certain level, but not to *learn* to play them at that level. This is and has to be nonsense. Indeed, anybody who plays an instrument at a high level of skill is in fact, and must be, constantly relearning to play it; that is to say, these coordinations must be resharpened every day.

My own experience with the cello convinces me

109

absolutely that if I could put the kind of time into the instrument, as I would dearly love to, that a serious young instrumentalist does, I could acquire a very high level of skill. I started the cello essentially at forty and played a couple of years and stopped for about eight years and began again very nearly from scratch at fifty, which was eight years ago. I'm a long way from being a virtuoso, but the quartet I'm playing in is now working on the Dvořák "American" Quartet, and Schubert's *Death and the Maiden*. I won't claim we sound like the Juilliard, but we're playing the music and it's not easy.

Nothing I have encountered in my own work in music has convinced me that if I could put in enough time I could not get to be about as good as I want to. I mean good enough to play well most of the great literature. I happen to have about an eighty-hour-a-week job, so I don't get as much time as I'd like.

The myth that if you don't start early, you might as well not start, tends to be a self-fulfilling prophecy. The music-making world that young people confront reminds me a lot of the world of school sports. After a lot of weeding out, in the end you've got a varsity with a few performers and an awful lot of people on the sidelines thinking, "Gee, it's too bad I wasn't good enough." We need to be careful about that. There seems to be an unspoken idea, in instruction of the young, that the people who start the fastest will go the farthest. But that's not only an unproven theory; it's not even a tested theory. The assumption that the steeper the learning curve, the higher it will go, is also unfounded. If we did things a little differently, we might find out that people whose learning curves were much slower might later on go up just as high or higher.

110

On Practice

I think we ought to abolish the word. It only makes trouble. A father once told me that his daughter likes to play the violin, but hates to practice. Why talk about "practice"? Why not just talk about playing the violin?

For a professional performer, the distinction between "playing" and "practicing" is perfectly clear. "Playing" is when you perform before other people, and "practicing" is when you get ready to do it. But this distinction is nonsense for amateurs. What do I do with my cello? I *play*. I don't spend part of my time getting ready to play it, and the rest of the time playing it. Some of the time I play scales or things like that; some of the time I play pieces that I am going to play with other people; some of the time I read new music; some of the time I improvise. But all of the time I am playing the cello.

One of the great things that my first teacher did for me was to get me started playing great music, even if it was much too hard for me. And one of my amusements now is playing the first dozen or so bars of *Schelomo*, which is a virtuoso piece, most of which I couldn't even touch. But there are parts of it I can play, and this is very exciting to me. For me there is no such thing as "practice." When I play the cello, I play the cello, and that's all there is to it.

When I think about the tyranny of practice and the myth of starting early, I think of my niece, who began playing the piano at nine. My sister paid for lessons, but made no attempt to make the child practice. On the whole, my niece played for perhaps a half hour a day, perhaps more some days, less others. About all my sister ever did in the way of coercion, if there had been a long spell of no playing at all, was to tell my niece that

111

she didn't need to take lessons if she didn't want to, but
that there was no use taking them if she didn't play in
between them; it was just discouraging to her teacher.
My niece stopped lessons about the time she entered
high school, where she was enormously involved with
a number of different kinds of activities. She continued
to play sporadically, rarely as long as three quarters of
an hour a day, and many days not at all. When she went
to college, she could not take her piano with her, and
for a couple of years had no access to one. Then later
she got some kind of electric piano, which she kept in
her room. I think there must have been very few years
during her entire growing up when she ever played as
much as an hour a day, and I doubt very much whether
the overall average for those years was as much as half
an hour a day. However, because when she played it
was because she wanted to, and because she is a very
musical and music-loving person, and also a very intense
kind of character, when she did play it was with the ut-
most concentration. After she left college, she went to
San Francisco, where she has lived for a few years now.

Last year I was visiting my sister when my niece came
home for Thanksgiving. I heard her playing the piano
in her room, sight-reading Brahms and Debussy, very
credibly and musically. She was playing not their hardest
pieces, but nothing they wrote is easy. Knowing how
little she had been playing, I was truly astonished. More
recently, she has been able to get her own piano, a good
one, where she lives in San Francisco, and now plays
three or more hours a day. One of the pieces she is
working on is Bela Bártók's Third Piano Concerto. I
have not heard her play it, but from all I know of her,
she would not be undertaking it if all she could do was
hack through it. Besides, she is living with other musicians, and they would not put up with it.

When I tell people about my niece, they often point

out that most children who are not "made" to practice don't reach any such high level. While they may be right, the same is true of children who *are* made to practice. We need to take serious account of the fact, well known to all musicians, that most children who have been to any great degree pushed into music, however skillful they may become at it, do not enjoy it very much. A number of my professional musician friends have said wistfully that they wished they loved music as much as I do. In Japan, except for a few children who go on into professional training and music-making, virtually *all* Suzuki violin students, most of whom started out at two or three, drop out of music completely by the age of fourteen. There apparently is little or no amateur music-making in Japan. What price is all that ability?

Suzuki

I first read about Dr. Shinichi Suzuki's work in Japan in an article in the *New York Times* years ago. The article said that one day it occurred to Suzuki that since all Japanese children had the intelligence and skill to accomplish the difficult task of learning to speak Japanese, they could, if they wanted to, learn to play the violin (Suzuki's own instrument) in the same way. Since he believed that children's lives would be much enriched by music, as his own had been, he set out to devise a way of learning the violin that would be as close as possible to the method children use to learn their own language. He realized that children had to hear a lot of other people's speech before they could make their own, and that they did a lot of speaking before they did any reading or writing. He also realized that children want very much to do what they see the

113

adults around them doing. From these sound insights he developed his method. If Japanese parents wanted their child to study violin by this method, when the child was still a baby they would begin to play at home, every day if possible, and many times each day, recordings played by expert players of some of the simple violin tunes that the child would later learn to play. Soon the child would come to know the tunes and think of them as his or hers. (Later experiments have shown that babies six months old or younger can learn tunes well enough to respond happily when they hear them played.)

When the child was about three, one of the parents, usually the mother, would begin taking violin lessons with a Suzuki teacher, *bringing her child with her*. At the teacher's house, the teacher would give the mother a violin, show her how to hold it, and then play one of the tunes that the child already knew. Then the teacher would show the mother how to play the tune—since it was the first, it would be simple enough so that she could learn to play it quickly. After the lesson the teacher would tell the mother to practice that little tune at home until the next lesson. This would go on for a few lessons, the child always going with the mother to the lesson. Then, in perhaps the third or fourth lesson, if the child were still really interested—for Suzuki insisted that he would not force children to play—the teacher would mysteriously produce from somewhere a tiny child-sized violin, asking the child, "Would you like to try it?" Yes, indeed! So the mother and child would go home together with their violins, and would play together the little tune they both knew. After a while, the mother, though she was still expected to listen to the child play and was required to come to the lessons, could if she wished stop playing herself— by this time, the child could go on alone. As time went on, the child would learn other tunes, and along with individual lessons would play in groups with other children, discovering with delight that they, too, knew the same tunes.

In the original method, only after children gained considerably fluency on the violin, and could play fairly complicated tunes, were they introduced to the written notes for the tunes that they already could play. Not for still some time, I'm not sure how long, would they start learning new tunes from written notes instead of by ear.

So much for the basic method, which seemed to me then, as it does now, in good accord with all I know about children's learning. The *Times* article went on to say that children were encouraged to experiment with their instruments, to make sounds both fast and slow, high and low—I remember it said that children were asked to make sounds "like an elephant" or "like a little mouse." It then said that all over Japan, hundreds of four-, five-, and six-year-old children taught by these methods gathered to play music by Vivaldi, Handel, and Bach.

A few years later, when a group of these children came to the New England Conservatory on a tour of the U.S., I was there to hear them, along with several hundred others, many of them music teachers. The children, perhaps twenty of them, came onstage, healthy, energetic, and happy. At the time I thought the average age of the children might be five or six; I now think they may have been a year or two older. Dr. Suzuki and a young assistant checked the tuning of the children's violins. We waited in great suspense. What would they play? Perhaps some of the slower and easier tunes of Vivaldi, Handel, or Bach? Dr. Suzuki gave the downbeat, and then away they went—playing not some easy tune but the Bach Double Concerto, in perfect tune, tempo, and rhythm, and with great energy and musicality. It was breathtaking, hair-raising. I could not have been more astonished if the children had floated up to the ceiling. Rarely in my life have I seen and heard anything so far beyond the bounds of what I would have thought possible.

During the question period, Dr. Suzuki told us (through his young interpreter) that the Japanese children we had heard were unusual in only two respects: their families could afford to pay for this trip to the U.S., and their mothers could go with them. But there were apparently many hundreds or even thousands of children in Japan who could play as well.

Before saying anything about Suzuki in this country I have to emphasize that all I know about Suzuki instruction *in Japan* came from the *Times* story and a couple of others, and from what I learned at this short meeting. It is possible that the picture of Suzuki instruction that I made in my mind out of these brief materials was far from accurate. What actually happened then, or happens now, in Suzuki classes in Japan, I don't know. What I can say with certainty is that from all I have seen, heard, and read of it, Suzuki instruction in the U.S. today is very far from the method that I have just described, and even farther from the method by which children learn to speak their own language. Suzuki instruction today is, in fact, very much like most school instruction. The material to be learned is broken down into many very small pieces; each one is supposed to be done perfectly before the next one is attempted; mistakes are corrected instantly, from the outside, by the teacher or parent; there is considerable pressure put on the children to "practice"; and children are given little room or encouragement, if any at all, to improvise and experiment with the instrument.

Some of the reasons for this probably have to do with the differences between Japanese and American family life and culture. Japanese women are much more likely to be at home with their children, and Japanese parents, if told by an expert that they must play recordings of simple violin tunes for several hours a day for years on end, are perhaps more likely to do so. To some extent, Dr. Suzuki surely had to modify his method, whatever it was, to take into account differences in American family life, in American adults' ideas about how to treat small children (we are generally much more severe with them than the Japanese), and in American music teachers' ideas about how music had to be taught.

It is also important to note that not all Suzuki teachers are alike, any more than are all Montessori teachers, or any kind of teachers. Some are more inventive and flexible than others; indeed, as happened with Montessori, some Suzuki teachers have already broken off from the rather rigid American organization and call themselves independent Suzuki teachers, to give themselves the freedom, if they wish, to modify the strict methods handed down from above. If I ever teach string playing to adults and/or children, as someday I hope to, I will certainly use Suzuki materials, but much of the time I will use them in my own way. The only way to find out what Suzuki instruction is like is to see the people doing it. I have seen some astonishingly bad teaching done under the name of Suzuki, and also some very good teaching.

On the whole, though, it is safe to say that Suzuki instruction in this country has become very rigid. And whether because of this or for other reasons, it certainly is not producing the kinds of results that we were told it once produced in Japan. Some very fine string players are coming out of Suzuki training, no question about it. But there are very few six-to-eight-year-old American children who can play the Bach Double Concerto. If you hear large numbers of Suzuki children playing in this country, what you are more likely to hear are simple variations of "Twinkle, Twinkle, Little Star," which (for good enough musical reasons) has become a kind of Suzuki national anthem. The organization and the method are certainly doing some good, but much less than they apparently once did in Japan and, what is more to the point, much less than they could do here if they really practiced what they preach—that is, helped children to learn music in the same way that they once learned their own language.

The fundamental insight of Suzuki, the living heart of his method, is that just as children learn to speak by trying—at first very clumsily—to make some of the speech they hear others making around them, so children can best learn to make music by trying to play on their instruments tunes they have heard many times and know.

Some Suzuki teachers may be in danger of losing the point of this fundamental insight. Children learning to speak do not learn to say one short word or phrase perfectly, then another word of phrase, and so on. They say a great many things, as many as they can, and with much use and practice learn to say them better and better. In their learning they advance not on a narrow front but on a very broad one, working on many different things at once. But it looks as if some Suzuki students are being taught to spend a long time learning to play one or two simple tunes "correctly" before moving on to something else. When I hear children doggedly sawing away at "Twinkle, Twinkle, Little Star," all in the first position and using only the lower half of their bows, I don't feel much of the spirit of excitement and adventure that I hear when children are learning to speak.

What then is so good about Suzuki materials and methods?

(1) The musical selections are very good. They are playable—not too hard and not too easy. They are fun to play, and, what is just as important for the parents who will have to hear them over and over again, they are fun (or at the very worst, at least tolerable) to hear. The children are very soon playing pieces written by the great masters. Some have objected that what the children play are simplified versions of what the composers wrote, but I have no objection to that. A child I know well has already moved from a simplified version of a Bach piece to one much closer to the real thing. It doesn't cause her any problems and I don't see why it should. She just thinks that a piece she already liked has become more interesting.

(2) There are recordings available of good performances of the music that the children will be playing. I suspect that most parents don't play these as much as they might; still, with these recordings you *can* do Suzuki as it was supposed to be done: that is, you can make it possible for your children to know these tunes *before* they start trying to play them, so that, as in learning to talk, they can correct their own mistakes rather than have parents or teachers do this for them. One of the things American Suzuki teachers do that may be a mistake is to put little pieces of tape on the violin (or viola or cello) fingerboard so that children (or their parents) can tell by looking at them where the fingers are supposed to go. This is musical nonsense; it is our *ears*, not our eyes, that are supposed to tell us where to put our fingers.

(3) The children become members of a musical community. In a performing art, like music, the uniform curriculum for which the schools so mistakenly strive in other areas actually makes sense. Wherever Suzuki children go, they will find that other Suzuki children at

about their level of skill know the same pieces, *so they can play them together*, which is fun for the children and, beyond that, is one of the chief joys of music. Learning a musical instrument, at least until you get good enough to play in a band or orchestra, used to be a rather lonely business for children. Now it doesn't have to be. Not only can the Suzuki teachers in a community have their pupils play together every week or so, but there are in addition even larger gatherings of children, often hundreds of them, at various Suzuki conferences. These can be enormously exciting to the children. The actual classes and workshops may or may not be interesting, but in between them the children can rush around and play with other children all the music they know. One mother of two very talented children, who has gone to several of these big get-togethers, says that the best things that happen there, as far as the children are concerned, are the things that are not planned—informal, spontaneous music-making with other children. For me this is a very important asset, and one that outweighs any objections I have to the program.

On a visit with friends in New York state, I went to two very interesting Suzuki events. First I heard a rehearsal of a string orchestra in which my friends' daughter Vita, age seven, was playing violin. The young conductor had written a short piece in three parts for them, and it was interesting to watch him help them put it together. Later we went to a formal recital. First a number of students, ranging from five-year-old beginners to very skillful teenagers, played solo pieces, or, in one case, a piece for three players. Then the small orchestra of which Vita was a member played, in unison, a number of standard Suzuki pieces.

Recitals of children can often be tense and unhappy affairs, but this one was pure pleasure. One thing helped to make it so; I don't know whether this is standard practice at Suzuki recitals everywhere, or an invention of this particular group. They did not start the recital with the youngest children and slowly work up to the experts; instead, they mixed beginners and experts more or less randomly. There was no feeling of stars, or competition; it was simply a group of children making music together for their pleasure and the pleasure of their parents and any others who might hear them.

One observation bothered me, however. None of the soloists, not even the very talented girl who played the entire middle movement of the Bruch G Minor Concerto, one of the great pieces of the Romantic repertory, were allowed to tune their own violins; all had to bring them up for one of the adult teachers to tune. I can understand this for the beginners; not only can they probably not hear accurate fifths (the strings of violins, violas, and cellos are tuned a fifth apart), but their hands are not strong enough to turn the pegs. But why should the advanced players not have tuned their own instruments? I have to assume they knew how.

Perhaps the Suzuki people felt that letting some children tune their instruments while making others bring theirs up for adults to tune might result in drawing just the kind of line between "good" and "bad" players that they did not wish to draw. If this was their idea, then a good case can be made for it. Yet it is most important for even young and inexperienced players to learn as soon as possible to tune their instruments accurately; it is a "basic skill" of string players. If we need to invent devices to make it possible for little children to do this, then let's get busy and invent them.

All in all, the Suzuki materials and organization can be a very useful resource—*one of many*—for children learning music, and for their parents (perhaps also learning music). The trick is to make use of those ma-

121

terials, but not restrict oneself to them. Branch out: encourage the children to improvise freely, to make up tunes, to write down tunes, to write compositions for each other to play, to begin as soon as possible to play real chamber music, which so far does not play a very big part in formal Suzuki instruction—though this may be changing, as it should be and as I hope it is.

In short, put back into learning music the exploration, the discovery, the adventure, and above all the joy and excitement that are properly a part of it, and that too formal and rigid instruction can only kill.

They've Got All the Exits Blocked

A friend of mine went to a school concert at which a string quartet was performing. The audience was fifth- or sixth-graders. As sometimes happens, there was one bunch of kids, bored and noisy and making various kinds of fuss. After a while, whoever was in charge told them they had to leave the room. As they left, my friend heard a child just in front of her say, "The luckies." This made me think of a story I read in *Symphony News*. The author, conductor of an orchestra that gave a lot of concerts in schools, reported that at one of these concerts, as he was coming near the stage, he came across a couple of boys in a corridor, and he heard one of them say to the other, "It's no use, we can't get out; they've got all the exits blocked." The author went on to say how splendid it was that these children were getting exposed to classical music! I wrote *Symphony News* that it seemed to me the author had gotten the wrong message from that exchange.

Many of my friends are professional musicians in the field we call classical. Every time they get together it seems to me that they spend a lot of time talking about ways to block more of the exits, to set up more compulsory exposure to music among young people. When I've had enough of this, I usually respond by asking them, "Do you want the schools to do for Beethoven and Mozart what they have already done for Shakespeare?" It rocks them back a little.

When I was traveling more, I used to hear quite a number of concerts and rehearsals in Indianapolis. The conductor there, Izler Solomon, was a marvelous musician and a great friend of mine. One evening, during an intermission, I fell into conversation with a man there whom I had seen before, a regular concertgoer. After he found out that I was a teacher and knew a lot of kids, he told me how he had been trying to get his children interested in coming to a concert. He said he had never been able to get them to come to hear the symphony. He said they just didn't seem to have any interest in good music. I said to him, "When you talk about symphonic music, these concerts, is that the phrase you use to describe it—'good music'?" And he said, "Yes." "Could I possibly persuade you," I said to him, "to call it something else?" He looked at me a second and then he began to chuckle. "Maybe I see what you mean," he said.

Feelings in Music

Another word that I want to get out of the vocabulary of music is *fun*. It is generally used in a negative sense, usually with some asperity, as in "Learning can't all be fun." What this conjures up is that proverbial scale of 1 to 10, or let's say −100 to +100, with "fun" on the +100 end of the scale, and "no fun" at the other end (as in "Gee, Ma, this is no fun," "Gee, Ma, why do I have to do this?"). The assumption is that while playing music we vary from the "no fun" end of the scale to the "fun" end. If we spend 99 percent of our time at the "no fun" end of the scale, eventually we will get to a point where we have a little fun. I think this is a disastrously mistaken way of looking at music. Nowhere on that scale of "no fun" to "fun" can I find any of the emotions that I feel when I am working with my cello. These range from arduous effort to intense concentration, great frustration and exasperation to something that can only be called exaltation. There are feelings so deep that one can barely play the music. You can't use the word *fun* to describe that range of feelings. Nor does the word convey the range of feelings that I observe in a five-year-old friend of mine when she plays her violin or piano.

Sometime in the last year she decided that she was going to play the violin and made this known to her nice parents, who got her one. She was already quite a remarkable beginning pianist. She is a small child, and to see these baby starfish hands thumping out a piece is almost beyond imagining. The volume of tone and sound that this mite produces on the piano when she plays with spirit is hard to describe. She and her very talented brother, about four years older, appear to experience feelings of excitement and passion on the one hand, and baffled fury on the other. Sometimes they just burst out crying, so furious that they can't get the phrase to come out the way they want it to. This five-year-old is not operating on an emotional range with "no fun" at one end and "fun" at the other. We trivialize music when we think in those terms. The effort, the concentration, the frustration, the doggedness, the resolution, the moments of surprise and joy—yes, the exaltation—are in another world altogether.

CHAPTER FIVE

What Parents Can Do

A veteran teacher summed it up
beautifully: "A word to the wise,"
he said, "is infuriating."

Grown-up Voices

When my sister and I were about four and five, perhaps even younger, we visited our grandparents. There was a landing on the second floor, with banisters through which we could just see down the stairs into the room where the adults sat talking after dinner. After we had been tucked into bed and good-nights said, and the grown-ups had gone back downstairs, we would slip out of bed, crouch down by the banisters, and listen to the grown-up voices. We couldn't catch more than a few of the words, and in any case couldn't understand what was being talked about. But the pull of those voices was fascinating. Usually after a while we would sneak back into bed. One night, however, we fell asleep there on the landing, where the grown-ups found us when they went up to bed. I don't remember what came of this, whether we were scolded or punished, and sternly warned not to get out of bed again, or whether the grown-ups said nothing about it.

Since then I have seen in many other families that it is very hard to keep young children in bed if a group of adults is having lively conversation not too far away. The children will find a hundred different reasons for coming to check out what the grown-ups are doing.

When I tell this story about my sister and me listening

eagerly at the top of the stairs and point out how much children can learn simply from adult conversation, parents or teachers will sometimes reply, "That's all very fine for privileged families that have interesting visitors. But what about most families, average families?" The answer is, first of all, that all people are interesting. As Studs Terkel and Robert Coles have shown in their (very different) books, everyone has many good stories to tell. As long as real people are talking, children will want to hear their voices and see their faces, and will learn much from them.

Uninvited Teaching

As far as learning goes, the one advantage we have over children—and in some ways it's a considerable advantage—is that we have been here longer. We know a lot more. We've had a lot more experience. We know where things are. We have road maps of the world, not just real road maps, but various mental road maps of the world around us.

What adults can do for children is to make more and more of that world and the people in it accessible and transparent to them. The key word is *access*: to people, places, experiences, the places where we work, other places we go—cities, countries, streets, buildings. We can also make available tools, books, records, toys, and other resources. On the whole, kids are more interested in the things that adults really use than in the little things we buy especially for them. I mean, anyone who has seen little kids in the kitchen knows that they would rather play with the pots and pans than anything made by Fisher-Price or Lego or name whomever you will.

We can also help children by answering their questions. However, all adults must be careful here, because we have a tendency, when a child asks us a question, to answer far too much. "Aha," we think, "now I have an opportunity to do some teaching," and so we deliver a fifteen-minute thesis for an answer. There is a well-known story about a child in school who was assigned to read a book on penguins and write a report on it. His book report had the usual stuff up in the corner: name, grade, school, class, subject, et cetera, and then the title of the book and the author and finally the body of the report, which read as follows: "This book tells me more about the penguins than I want to know."

Whenever a child asks questions, there's a danger to, one might say, penguinize. I heard a similar story about a child who asked her mother some question and the mother was busy or distracted, or perhaps didn't feel she knew enough, and said, "Why don't you ask your father?" The child replied, "Well, I don't want to know that much about it." If children want more, they'll ask for more. The best we can do is simply to answer the specific question and if we don't know the answer say, "I don't know, but maybe we can find it somewhere or so-and-so might know."

Not only is it the case that uninvited teaching does not make learning, but—and this was even harder for me to learn—for the most part such teaching prevents learning. Now that's a real shocker. Ninety-nine percent of the time, teaching that has not been asked for will not result in learning, but will impede learning. With a minimum of observation, parents will find this confirmed all the time. Again and again, in letters and conversations, I hear from parents a story that goes as follows: "My little two-year-old (or three- or four-) was having some kind of problem with something the other day and I went over to help her or him and the child turned on me with rage and said, 'Leave me alone. Don't do it. Let me do it!' The child got absolutely furious.

128

What happened?" These poor, helpful, well-meaning mothers and fathers reel back from this assault and say, "Why does my child get so furious at me when all I want to do is help?" Well, there is a reason, a very sensible reason.

Anytime that, without being invited, without being asked, we try to teach somebody else something, anytime we do that, we convey to that person, whether we know it or not, a double message. The first part of the message is: I am teaching you something important, but you're not smart enough to see how important it is. Unless I teach it to you, you'd probably never bother to find out. The second message that uninvited teaching conveys to the other person is: What I'm teaching you is so difficult that, if I didn't teach it to you, you couldn't learn it.

This double message of distrust and contempt is very clearly understood by children, because they are extremely good at receiving emotional messages. It makes them furious. And why shouldn't it? All uninvited teaching contains this message of distrust and contempt. Once I realized this, I found that I had to catch myself all the time. I have to catch the words right on the edge of my tongue. The problem is that we human beings like teaching. We're a teaching animal, as well as a learning animal. We have to restrain that impulse, that habit, that need to explain things to everybody . . . unless we are asked.

The Power of Example

Often, when small children become bored and distracted, at home or in nursery school, adults will decide that they "need more structure." I tend to be wary of that term, since those who use it generally mean only one thing: some adult standing over the child telling him what to do and making sure he does it.

Many young children do indeed need to be introduced to tasks and activities that take time, concentration, effort, and skill. But this isn't a matter of "giving" harder tasks and making the child persist until he or she is finished. In such situations the controlling factor is the will of the adult, not, as it should be, *the requirements of the task*. Instead, what young children need is the opportunity to see older children and adults choosing and undertaking various tasks and working on them over a period of time until they are completed. Children need to get some sense of the *processes* by which good work is done. The only way they can learn how much time and effort it takes to build, say, a table, is to be able to see someone building a table, from start to finish. Or painting a picture. Or repairing a bicycle, or writing a story, or whatever it may be.

At the Ny Lille Skole, the wonderful small school in Denmark about which I have often written, the six adult "teachers" had all done many kinds of work before they began teaching, and all brought to the school a number of visible and interesting skills. One woman was a good musician and dancer, another a skilled weaver, several of the men were good at working with tools in both wood and metal. One teacher was actually making himself a bass viol at the school. It took a long time: it was a serious instrument. Some of the older kids worked with him on the project; younger kids hung around, helped a little, asked questions; still younger children watched less attentively, for shorter stretches of time. But even the youngest children were aware of that project going on, and kept track of its progress.

Children need to see things done well. Cooking, and especially baking, where things change their texture and shape (and taste yummy), are skills that children might

130

like to take part in. Typing might be another, and to either or both of these could be added bookmaking and bookbinding. These are crafts that children could take part in from beginning to end. Skilled drawing and painting or woodworking might be others.

Adults must use the skills they have where children can see them. In the unlikely event that they have no skills to speak of, they should learn some, and let the children see them learning, even if only as simple a thing as touch typing. They should invite children to join them in using these skills. In this way children can be slowly drawn, at higher and higher levels of energy, commitment, and skill, into more and more serious and worthwhile adult activities.

When parents point out to me that their work is not as impressive in its progress as, say, that of a boat builder, I use my own work as an example. While writing is less easy to understand than the work of a carpenter or farmer, it is not necessarily opaque or meaningless to a child. Writing is a process that takes place in time. I begin with raw materials and scraps of notes, write rough drafts, correct them, change them, finally produce a smooth draft, turn this over to someone else for further editing, and see it go into galleys or some kind of proof sheets and eventually find its way into the finished newspaper, magazine, or book. Even if what I write about might not make much sense to children, they will surely be interested in many of the things I actually do. At every stage of the process outlined above, parents who are writers might show their child what they have done and talk a little (as much as the child wants) about what they are going to do next, and why. In the end, they could show the child their articles when they finally appear in print. They might even keep all their notes and rough drafts for a particular article, and on a big piece of cardboard paste up an exhibit showing everything from the first steps to the final product. This would also be an easy and interesting thing to do in schools; it would show students what none of them now know or could imagine—the amount of work that goes into serious writing.

It is this sense of *process over time* that children want and need to learn about, and much of this is visible in most kinds of work. Even if parents can't show children their actual workplace, they can show them similar places. For instance, for the child of a journalist, any small offset press would be fascinating: the noise, all those things going round and round, the paper flying out with stuff printed on it. A mystery! But children would see that a grown-up understands it and controls it, and thinks that maybe someday, if they wanted, they could too. They would also learn that their parents did not think of them as too small and stupid to be included in a central part of their own lives.

Teaching as a Natural Science

Helping children explore and learn in the world is best seen as a branch of natural science, like trying to raise exotic plants or little-known animals, or perhaps trying to establish communication with dolphins and whales. What is called for and needed is something that very few teachers (unlike great naturalists) have, which is the ability to observe very closely and accurately, with a great eye for detail, and to report very accurately what is seen. In the mid-nineteenth century, the zoologist Louis Agassiz began a college course by putting a fish on a plate and asking his students to describe it. Every time they thought they had said all there was to say, and brought their papers up to him, he only said, "What else?" He did not let them stop looking at and writing about that fish until they had seen in it a hundred times more than they would have guessed there was to be seen. It is this ability to see, and then describe accurately what was seen, that is the hallmark of the great naturalists, and a necessity for good teaching.

While such close, patient observation is rare in most teachers, it comes more easily to parents, because of their interest in, and love for, their children. Like a naturalist, an observant parent will be alert both to small clues and to large patterns of behavior. By noticing these, a parent can often offer appropriate suggestions and experiences, and also learn whether the help and explanations already given have been adequate.

Children have their own styles of learning, every one unique. They also have their own timetables, according to which they are ready to do things, speeds at which they want to do them, and time they want to wait before doing a new thing. When we try to direct, or interfere with, or change these learning styles and timetables, we almost always slow or stop them. It is much easier to see this in young children because the things they are learning are so visible—simple skills, names of letters, new words. If Billy has been asking us the names of letters when he sees them and, because we start quizzing him, suddenly stops, we can see that he has stopped. In young children changes of behavior are large and obvious. Also, they have not learned and do not try to conceal their acts and thoughts and feelings. (These are actually all one, experienced as one by children and all healthy people of any age.) Older children may learn to hide from us, trick us. Because of fear, even first-graders become adept at concealment and learn evasive strategies. When I wrote *How Children Fail*, it was only after months of observing and keeping careful notes that I was able to see underlying patterns of self-defeating behavior that the fifth-graders in my class had learned to conceal.

In trying to help small children, adults—whether nursery-school teachers, parents, or friends of these children—might look to the great natural scientists who have followed in Louis Agassiz's footsteps: Konrad Lorenz, Niko Tinbergen, Jane Goodall, or E. O. Wilson. Or they might look to the children themselves. "Science," of course, is not the private property of "scientists," but something that we all do when we are trying to solve some kind of problem or puzzle. Children, as I mentioned earlier, are acting like scientists all the time, which is to say looking, noticing, wondering, theorizing, testing their theories, and changing them as often as they have to.

Whose Right Hand?

In making a mental model of the world, among the labels a small child must learn are "right" and "left." Most children learn them easily. They would hardly be worth mentioning, except for the fact that schools get very upset and anxious about them. As I wrote in *Teach Your Own*, if a child writes a letter backward, or reads off some letters in the wrong order, or does anything else to suggest he is confused about right and left, adults begin to talk excitedly about "mixed dominance" and "perceptual handicaps" and "learning disabilities." Specialists are called in and told to take over.

Once in an early elementary classroom, I needed something in my desk, and asked a child if he would get it for me. He said OK, and asked where it was. I said, "In the top right-hand drawer." There was a pause. Then he said, "Whose right hand, mine or the desk's?"

For a second, I was baffled. What on earth could he mean? Then I saw, and understood. When he looked at the desk, it was as if he saw a living creature facing him. So I said, "Your right hand." Off he went, brought back what I had asked for, and that was that.

Later it occurred to me that many young children must be animists, and see objects as if they were living creatures. I wondered how many of them might have had that same question in their minds, without ever getting around to asking it. How did they ever learn the answer? I decided after a while that one way or another they learned it from experience. They went to the desk, looked in *its* right-hand drawer, found nothing, looked in *their* right-hand drawer, found what they wanted, and so learned which was meant. I realized that these children used the same approach as a toddler whom I described in *How Children Learn*. While sitting at the dinner table, she asked people to pass her the salt, pepper, butter, and so on, so that she could find out what those words meant.

But some children might not react that way. They might assume that the adult had made a mistake about the drawer. Or they might think that they themselves had made a mistake about which was right and which was left. The kind of children who *worry about mistakes* (because their parents or teacher worry) might be particularly ready to blame themselves for any confusion.

Most children master the confusion of right and left because they never actually become aware of it, any more than I did until recently. Others may become aware of the confusion but are not troubled by it and don't feel any need to set it right or make sense of it— it's just the way things are. But some children are philosophers. They examine everything. They like things

135

to make sense, and if they don't (which our right-left rules do not), to find out why not. Still others are threatened and terrified. I suspect that most of the children who have persistent trouble with right and left in school or in life are of this latter kind. After a few right-left mistakes, which they make only because they have not yet learned our crazy right-left rules, they begin to think, "I must be stupid. I never can figure out right and left." Soon they go into a blind panic every time the words come up. They work out complicated strategies of bluff and avoidance. When people ask about right and left, they learn to get other clues. ("You mean the one over there by the window?")

How could such children be helped? One thing we should not do, which the schools are very likely to do if they ever buy this theory of mine, is to set out to teach the "rules" of right and left, as they now teach the "rules of phonics," or colors or shapes or sounds, as if no one ever learned anything unless it was taught. I can just see workbooks with lists of things that have their own right hands, and things that do not, with daily tests for the children, and so on.

Most children have always figured out right and left without much teaching, other than being told when very little, "This is your right hand; this is your left." Let them go on learning that way. But if a child seems to be confused or anxious about this, then we can be more explicit. We can say, "I mean *your* right hand, not the desk's," or "I mean the *coat's* right hand, not yours," perhaps adding, "I know that sounds a little crazy, but that's just the way we do it; don't worry about it, you'll get used to it."

In my mind's eye I can also see a little right-left reminder—a little rug, or piece of heavy cloth, or wood, or even cardboard, with an outline of the child's two bare feet, side by side, the right foot marked *R*, and the left *L*. When the child stands on it, with his feet pointed the same way, he can then tell which is which.*

Correcting Mistakes

When children first learn to talk, they will often use the name of one object to refer to a whole class of similar objects. In *How Children Learn*, I told of a child who called all animals in fields "cows," even horses and sheep. There are a number of important reasons why I feel strongly that not correcting such "mistakes" is the proper thing to do.

(1) Courtesy: if a distinguished person from a foreign country were visiting you, you would not correct every mistake he made in English, however much he might want to learn the language, because it would be rude. We do not think of rudeness or courtesy as being applicable to our dealings with very little children. But they are.

(2) The child who first isolates a class of objects and labels them has performed a considerable intellectual feat. Our first reaction to any such feat should be one of acceptance and recognition. Without making a great to-do about it, we should by our actions make clear to the child that he has accomplished something good, not that he has made a mistake. Put yourself in his position. If you were just learning, in a foreign country, to speak a foreign language, how would you feel if everyone around you corrected every error you made? Unless you are a most exceptional person, the effect of this would be to make you so careful that you would wind up saying little or nothing—like a man I know who,

---

* A similar discussion of how children learn left from right appeared in *Teach Your Own* (New York: Delacorte Press, 1981).

after six or seven winters in Mexico, cannot speak twenty words of Spanish because he can't bring himself to say anything unless he is sure he is right.

(3) Some would say, "We do not help if we do nothing or say nothing to facilitate learning." But that is the point. Just by our using the language ourselves, we give the child all the help she needs. Because other people called some of these animals "horses" or "sheep" instead of "cows," this little child learned, and very quickly, that this is what they were called. In short, we do not need to "teach" or "correct" in order to help a child learn.

(4) It is always, without exception, better for a child to figure out something on his own than to be told— provided, of course, as in the matter of running across the street, that his life is not endangered in the learning. But in matters intellectual, I admit no exception to this rule. In the first place, what he figures out, he remembers better. In the second place, and far more important, every time he figures something out, he *gains confidence in his ability to figure things out.*

(5) We are fooling ourselves if we think that by being nice about it we can prevent corrections from sounding like reproofs. It is only in exceptional circumstances and with the greatest tact that you can correct an adult without to some degree hurting his or her feelings. How can we suppose that children, whose sense of identity or ego or self-esteem is so much weaker, can accept correction equably? I would say that in ninety-nine cases out of a hundred, any child will take correction as a kind of reproof, and this no matter how enthusiastic, pleasant, relaxed, or stimulating we may happen to be. I am ready to be about as dogmatic about this as about anything I know of; I have seen it too often with my own eyes.

(6) It is true, in a way, and misleading, in a way, to say that children want to learn. Yes, they do, but in the

way that they want to breathe. Learning, no more than breathing, is not an act of volition for young children. They do not think, "Now I am going to learn this or that." It is in their nature to look about them, to take the world in with their senses, and to make sense of it, without knowing at all how they do it or even that they are doing it. One of the greatest mistakes we make with children is to make them self-conscious about their learning, so that they begin to ask themselves, "Am I learning or not?" The truth is that anyone who is really *living*, exposing himself or herself to life and meeting it with energy and enthusiasm, is at the same time learning. It is worrying about learning that turns off children's learning. When they begin to see the world as a place of danger, from which they must shut themselves off and protect themselves, when they begin to live less freely and fully, that is when their learning dies down.

(7) Even when children reach the age when they are, some of the time, self-consciously and deliberately learning something that they want to learn, it does not follow that they always want to be told. A healthy child will almost always rather figure something out for herself. A veteran teacher not long ago summed it up beautifully. "A word to the wise," he said, "is *infuriating*."

Praise Junkies

There has been much written about how important it is to encourage children's self-concept by giving them lots of praise. To me, this advice is a serious mistake. I feel strongly about this issue because my first elementary-school teaching was at a school that believed in supporting children with lots of praise. By the time I came to know them in fifth grade, all but a few

139

en were so totally dependent on continued
val that they were terrified of not getting it,
of making mistakes. The practice of that
and since then I have seen many others like
exactly the *opposite* results from those in-
te... Every teacher in that school was intent upon
nurturing each child's self-esteem, but despite their in-
tentions, their stream of praise had an extremely destructive effect on most of the children. Though affluent,
high-I.Q., and favored in all possible ways, they were
pathetically lacking in self-confidence.

Since then, I have seen a great many adults working
with children, in school and other settings, and I would
say that something like 99 percent of the praise I have
observed was more harmful than helpful. I think of
countless teenagers I have known who hated themselves despite having been praised all their lives. They
say, "People just praised me to get me to do what they
wanted." Many children are both cynical about praise
and dependent on it, the worst possible mixture.

The trouble with any kind of external motivation,
whether it be negative (threats or punishments or
scoldings) or positive (gold stars, M&M's, grades, Ph.D.'s
or Phi Beta Kappa keys), is that it displaces or sub-
merges internal motivation. Babies do not learn in order
to please us, but because it's their instinct and nature
to want to find out about the world. If we praise them
for everything they do, after a while they are going to
start learning, doing things, just to please us, and the
next step is that they are going to become worried
about not pleasing us. They're going to become just as
afraid of doing the wrong thing as they might have been
if they had been faced with the threat of punishment.

What children want and need from us is thoughtful
attention. They want us to notice them and pay some
kind of attention to what they do, to take them seriously,

to trust and respect them as human beings. They want courtesy and politeness, but they don't need much praise.

Unwanted Help

Something happened a while ago in the office that showed me once again how intense and yet how fragile little children's sense of pride and dignity is, and how careful we must be not to trample on it, most of all when we mean well.

A mother came into the office with her eighteen-month-old daughter. While the mother looked over our books to see what she wanted to buy, the little one explored the office. Finally the mother had the four books she wanted, which the little girl asked to carry. But one of the books kept slipping out from between the others and falling to the ground, and this began to frustrate and irritate the child. Seeing that she clearly did not like having the book fall on the floor, I thought I might help by putting a rubber band around them. I got a rubber band, stretched it a couple of times to show the little girl what it was, and put it around the books. She looked at it a second, saw that it was indeed holding the books together, and then burst into furious tears.

From many years of being with little children, I had a sense of what the matter was. She saw my putting the rubber band around the books as a comment, which indeed it was, on the fact that she could not hold them together, and she was offended. To her, it was as if I had said, "You're so clumsy that you'll never be able to carry those books unless I put this rubber band on." Quite naturally, this made her ashamed and angry.

Since I understood what the trouble was, I was able

141

to set things right. I said, "I'm sorry, I'll take that rubber band off," and did so. Instantly she stopped crying and was as happy as she had been before—not too happy, as a matter of fact, because she was getting hungry and was beginning to fuss a little about getting something to eat.

Thinking this over, I don't feel that I necessarily made a mistake in trying to help with the rubber band. It didn't bother me that she kept dropping the book, but I could see that it bothered her. Under other circumstances, perhaps in a place where she felt more at home, or at a time when she was not hungry and a little irritable, or even if she had known me a little better, she might have been willing and happy to accept the rubber-band solution to the book problem, might even have become interested in the rubber band, experimented with it, and played games with it.

But as it was, hungry, a little ill at ease in a strange place and before a strange (if friendly) man, exasperated by the trouble she had been having with the books, she took the offer of help as an insult. No harm was done; I quickly withdrew and canceled my "help," and, seeing her feelings and wishes understood and respected, she instantly forgave me and went on with life as before. What would have made the situation worse, and might have brought on a real crying fit, a "tantrum," as the detestable word goes, would have been my trying to ignore and override her feelings and her protest, insisting on solving the problem my way, perhaps even getting a little angry at her for rejecting my well-meant "help."

A letter I received from the mother of four young sons made the dangers of well-meaning but uninvited help dramatically clear. She had bought a large jigsaw puzzle for her boys, a map of the world, which came accompanied by a teacher's manual. As a dutiful parent

The Nature of Learning

Helping children explore and
learn in the world is best seen as
a branch of natural science, like
trying to raise exotic plants or
little-known animals.

Three Misleading Metaphors

More than we may realize, what we do in our lives and our work is greatly influenced by metaphors—the pictures we have in our minds about how the world works or ought to work. Often these images are more real to us than reality itself.

Organized education is governed and dominated by three particular metaphors. Some educators are more or less aware that their work is guided by these metaphors, others are not aware at all, and still others might vigorously deny their influence. But conscious or not, these metaphors have largely determined and still determine what most teachers do in school.

The first of these metaphors presents education as an assembly line in a bottling plant or canning factory. Down the conveyor belts come rows of empty containers of sundry shapes and sizes. Beside the belts is an array of pouring and squirting devices, controlled by employees of the factory. As the containers go by, these workers squirt various amounts of different substances—reading, spelling, math, history, science—into the containers.

Upstairs, management decides when the containers should be put on the belt, how long they should be left on, what kinds of materials should be poured or squirted into them at what times, and what should be done about containers whose openings (like pop bottles') seem to be smaller than the others, or seem to have no openings at all.

When I discuss this metaphor with teachers, many laugh and seem to find it absurd. But we need only to read the latest rash of school-improvement proposals to see how dominant this metaphor is. In effect, those official reports all say, we must have so many years of English, so many years of math, so many years of foreign language, so many years of science. In other words, we must squirt English into these containers for four years, math for two or three, and so on. The assumption is that whatever is squirted *at* the container will go *into* the container and, once in, will stay in.

No one seems to ask the obvious question: How come so many of the containers, having had these substances squirted at them for so many years, are still going out of the factory empty? In the face of a century of contrary experience, educators cling to the notion that teaching produces learning, and therefore, the more taught, the more learned. Not one of the reports I have read has raised serious questions about this assumption. If students don't know enough, we insist, it is because we didn't start squirting soon enough (start them at four), or didn't squirt the right stuff, or enough of it (toughen up the curriculum).

A second metaphor depicts students in a school as laboratory rats in a cage, being trained to do some kind of trick—most often a trick that no rat in real life would ever have any reason to perform. Here sits the rat and at the other end of the cage is a circular shape and a triangular shape. If the rat presses the "right" shape—the one the experimenter wants him to press—out comes a tasty morsel. If the rat presses the "wrong" shape, the unwanted one, he gets an electric shock. According to John Goodlad of the School of Education

149

at the University of California in Los Angeles, this is what almost all teaching in schools was at the turn of the century, and it is still what teaching is today—task, morsel, shock. For morsel and shock, read carrot and stick, or "positive reinforcement" and "negative reinforcement."

The positive reinforcements in schools are teachers' smiles, gold stars, A's on report cards, dean's lists, and, at the end, entrance into prestigious colleges, good jobs, interesting work, money, and success. The negative reinforcements are angry scoldings, sarcasm, contempt, humiliation, shame, the derisive laughter of other children, the threats of failure, of being held back, of flunking out of school. For many poor children, the negative reinforcements include physical beatings. At the end of this line are entrance into low-rank colleges or none at all, bad jobs or none at all, dull work if any, not much money or outright poverty.

The third metaphor is, perhaps, the most destructive and dangerous of all. It describes the school as a mental hospital, a treatment institution. Schools, top-rank or low-rank, have always operated under the wonderfully convenient rule that when learning takes place, the school deserves the credit ("If You Can Read, Thank a Teacher"); and that when it doesn't, the students get the blame. The blame used to be parceled out in plain English. At a highly rated private elementary school, a veteran teacher put it this way: "If the children don't learn what we teach, it's because they're lazy, disorganized, or mentally disturbed," and all but a few of his colleagues agreed.

More recently, however, educators have found another explanation for lack of learning: "learning disabilities." This explanation became popular because it had something for almost everyone. Guilt-ridden middle-class parents of failing students could stop asking, "What did we do wrong?" The experts told them, "You didn't do anything wrong; your child's just got some wires crossed in his head." Angry people demanding that schools "get busy and teach my kid something" could be told, "I'm sorry, there's nothing we can do; he's learning disabled."

Children as young as five or six, often in their first days at school, are now routinely given batteries of tests "to find out what is wrong with them." Some children are even *told* by their teachers that this is what the tests are for. A substantial part of the pseudoscience of pedagogy is now made up of listing and describing these diseases, the tests that are supposed to diagnose them, and the activities designed to treat but hardly ever designed to cure.

The "research" behind these labels is biased and not very persuasive. Some years ago, at a large conference of specialists in learning disability, I asked whether anyone had ever heard of—not done, but merely heard of—any research linking so-called perceptual handicaps with stress. In the audience of about 1,100, two hands were raised. One man told me then, the other told me later, about research that showed that when students with supposedly severe learning disabilities were put in a relatively stress-free situation, their disabilities soon vanished.

Our third metaphor, like the first two, presents a false picture of reality. The schools assume that children are not interested in learning and are not much good at it, that they will not learn unless made to, that they cannot learn unless shown how, and that the way to make them learn is to divide up the prescribed material into a sequence of tiny tasks to be mastered one at a time, each with its appropriate morsel and shock. And when this method doesn't work, the schools assume there is something wrong with the children—something they must try to diagnose and treat.

All these assumptions are wrong. If you start from Chicago to go to Boston, and you think that Boston is due west of Chicago, the farther you go, the worse off you will be. If your assumptions are wrong, your actions will be wrong, and the harder you try, the worse off you will be.

The easily observable fact is that children are passionately eager to make as much sense as they can of the world around them, are extremely good at it, and do it as scientists do, by *creating* knowledge out of experience. Children observe, wonder, find, or make and then test the answers to the questions they ask themselves. When they are not actually *prevented* from doing these things, they continue to do them and to get better and better at it.*

Learning Is Making Sense of Things

Children are much more able than we think to recognize when one thing they've said, or that somebody has said, isn't quite consistent with another. In other words, they want the parts of their mental model to fit. If the parts don't fit, they're disturbed. They are, in a sense, philosophers; they like to resolve contradictions. They're made uneasy by paradox. They like to have things make sense. But they have to do this in their own way and in their own time.

Until a child becomes really dissatisfied with his own mental model, until he feels it isn't right, corrections don't make sense. They roll right off his back. Correc-

* Portions of this section appeared in *The Progressive* (April 1984).

tions that he makes, or at least is in the mood to listen to, are the corrections that he needs.

The reason why teaching in the conventional sense of the word—telling children things—is almost inherently impossible, is that we cannot know what the state of a young child's mind is. He hasn't got words to tell us. All of us know more than we can say—and I don't just mean more than we have time to say—more than we can put into words. But this is one hundred times more true of a child: he has a great many more understandings that he cannot possibly verbalize, and a great many misunderstandings.

In his mental model of the world, there are a great many gaps that he might sense, but he is not able to put these into words. A child just feels a gap in his mind, like a missing piece in a jigsaw puzzle. But when, through his experiences, one way or another, along comes the piece of information that fits that gap, it's pulled in there as if by a magnet. I think we've all experienced this.

There's some little gap in our knowledge or understanding, and, all of a sudden, perhaps in a book, perhaps out of some experience, there comes an idea and it fits. You practically feel it rush into the hole and you plug it up tight. You don't forget things like that. These are the sorts of things kids learn. They can't tell us what these things are. They have no way of telling.

If a child is left alone with a pile of books or material, 95 percent of what she reads goes into her head—and right out again. But when she is doing this on her own, what happens is like what happens in one of these chemical plants that get magnesium out of seawater. Billions of gallons go pouring through this great conversion plant. They don't get much magnesium out of a gallon of seawater, but an enormous number of gallons go through. This, I think, is true of children.

When a child is learning on his own, following his own curiosity, an enormous amount of stuff is going through the plant. From this he is picking out subconsciously the stuff he needs. What we do when we try to decide everything for him is to slow down the process without increasing the efficiency. We think we're making it more efficient—but we're really not. We're just cutting down the intake.

What is efficient? How does a small child learn language? She absorbs with her ears an enormous amount of verbal information—if she is living in a family where she hears a lot of talk and where people talk to her. Most of it she doesn't remember or doesn't even understand. But she picks out a bit here, a bit there. She picks out the things she wants and needs. We say, "Ha, this is inefficient. When we get her in school, we're going to show her the efficient way to study language." We have grammar, our tenses, vocabulary lists. But which is more efficient? Who learns languages better?

One of my objections to school is that the kind of child who, for reasons of personal integrity—really wants to do what we're telling him, really wants to learn and not just pass an exam—gets into endless trouble because he is the kind of student who is always asking questions. The teacher thinks, "I've got all this material to cover. I don't want to go into the whys and wherefores." This kind of student, being something of a philosopher, will be very conscious of contradictions and paradoxes because life is full of them.

Maybe the best minds in the field are trying to resolve his conflicts. Poor Miss Jones isn't going to be able to resolve them, and she doesn't want to be heckled by them. This kind of kid gets little help in school. He's in hot water. He learns very quickly that nobody is interested in having him understand how these things really work.

Over the years, I have noticed that the child who learns quickly is adventurous. She's ready to run risks. She approaches life with arms outspread. She wants to take it all in. She still has the desire of the very young child to make sense out of things. She's not concerned with concealing her ignorance or protecting herself. She's ready to expose herself to disappointment and defeat. She has a certain confidence. She expects to make sense out of things sooner or later. She has a kind of trust.

On the other hand, to the less successful student, the world is not only a somewhat senseless place, it's tricky. It's her enemy to some extent. She doesn't know what is going to happen, but she has a pretty good hunch it's going to be bad. She is not trusting.

The successful student is resourceful, and he's also patient. He'll try something one way, and if he doesn't get it, OK, he'll try it this way, and if that doesn't work, he'll try it another. But the unsuccessful student has neither the resourcefulness to think of many ways nor the patience to hang on.

The good student, possibly because he's not so worried, possibly because he has this style of thinking, is able to look objectively at his own work—to stand back from it and to look for inconsistency and to see mistakes. *This can't be right if this is right. So, let's see what's wrong here.*

Adults have to be conscious of a rise and fall in children—like the rise and fall of the tide—of courage and confidence. Some days kids have a tiger in their tank. They're just raring to go; they're full of enthusiasm and confidence. If you knock them down, they bounce up. Other days, you scratch them and they pour out blood. What you can get them to try, and what you can get them to tolerate in the way of correction or advice, depends enormously on how they feel, on how big their store of confidence and self-respect happens to be at the moment. This may vary—it may vary even within the space of an hour.

If you don't punish a child when she isn't feeling brave, pretty soon she will feel brave. That is, if you don't outrun her store of courage, she will get braver.

A child only pours herself into a little funnel or into a little box when she's afraid of the world—when she's been defeated. But when a child is doing something she's passionately interested in, she grows like a tree—in all directions. This is how children learn, how children grow. They send down a taproot like a tree in dry soil. The tree may be stunted, but it sends out these roots, and suddenly one of these little taproots goes down and strikes a source of water. And the whole tree grows.

One of the things you find in listening to the conversations of children is that the questions that little kids ask themselves about the world are likely to be very big questions, not little ones. They don't ask, "Why does the water come out of the tap?" Instead they ask, "Where did the universe come from?"

Children are not only philosophers; they are cosmologists, they're inventors of myths, of religions—literally. Like the Indians who came up with the idea that there was a turtle and the world grew out of his back, or that the gods brought fire.

We tend to be patronizing or to take a precious view of children's fantasies and stories. "That's a lovely story, Jimmy, but of course you know it isn't true." But this is a child engaged in a very serious work. He's not just diverting himself—he's trying to make a model of the universe, really on a much bigger scale than you or I ever think on anymore. He's asking himself questions about time and life and God and creation. These are philosophers at work. We should give them time to think.*

Living as Learning

Not long ago I heard a college president refer to himself as a "womb-to-tomber": that is, a person who would like us all to be learners all our lives. What he actually meant, of course, was that he would like us to be students at some educational institution, with or without walls, all our lives. He meant that he would like us to be responsible to some expert or body of experts for what we know, that we would for all our lives be in the position of having to prove every so often that we were shaping up, knowing a satisfactory amount of what these experts felt we ought to know. Horrifying as I found this statement, it made me think that in a properly understood sense we are *already* learners all our lives. Living is learning. It is impossible to be alive and conscious (and some would say unconscious) without constantly learning things. If we are alive we are receiving various sorts of messages from our environment all the time. We take these in in one form or another and make use of them. We are constantly experiencing reality and in one way or another incorporating it into our mental model of the universe: the organized sum of what we think we know about everything. Many people, in order to protect the integrity of their rather simple mental

* Adapted from an interview in *Grade Teacher* (1966).

model, in order to save themselves the pain of having to rethink things they thought they understood, react to any experiences that do not conform with what they think they already know, do not fit neatly into the already existing mental model, by rejecting these experiences. Yet even this is to add something to the mental model.

Let us imagine that two people read in a newspaper or magazine an article that gravely shakes up or contradicts their notions of how things really are. One of these people confronts this new experience squarely, does not reject it, tries to fit it into his model or rather readjust his model to take account of it—always a slow and painful experience and one I'm always in the middle of. The other person, in an approach we often call narrowminded, may just reject that piece of information altogether. But he does not leave the experience where he came in. He must somehow or other account for the fact of its having been in the newspaper. So he makes up a theory that somebody was lying to the paper, or, more probably, that the paper is lying to him, perhaps that it is run by Communists or perverts or something. Maybe he adds a couple of more names to his list of people or publications that he will not believe.

In the same way we learn something from any and all kinds of experiences in our lives. If we live in or go to a city, and see all kinds of beautiful buildings, fascinating places, and activities, we learn from what we see. We learn that cities can be interesting, and perhaps we get some ideas about what we might do to make other cities more livable and interesting. If, on the other hand, we go to a city and are frightened or bored or disgusted with what we see, we may learn nothing pleasant, but we do learn not only that the city is bad but that probably most cities are. Perhaps we learn, like many people, to hate cities in general.

158

If we meet an interesting new person, we learn a great deal about that person and his or her life and interests. He or she throws a light on many parts of the world that we did not know about, and we may incorporate some of them into our model and feel an urge to explore still further. If the person is not interesting, we may not learn anything else from him or her, but we at least learn that he or she is not interesting, and we may generalize from that to think that most people are not very interesting or that it is a good idea to stay away from parties or whatever it was where we met this not-interesting person. In the same way we learn something from the work we do, however interesting or dull, good or bad, it might be. It is not possible to be alive and conscious without learning something.

Every Waking Hour

A mong the many things I have learned about children, learned by many, many years of hanging out with them, watching carefully what they do, and thinking about it, is that children are natural learners.

The one thing we can be sure of, or surest of, is that children have a passionate desire to understand as much of the world as they can, even what they cannot see and touch, and as far as possible to acquire some kind of skill, competence, and control in it and over it. Now this desire, this need to understand the world and be able to do things in it, the things the big people do, is so strong that we could properly call it biological. It is every bit as strong as the need for food, for warmth, for shelter, for comfort, for sleep, for love. In fact, I think a strong case could be made that it might be stronger than any of these.

A hungry child, even a tiny baby who experiences

hunger as real pain, will stop eating or nursing or drinking if something interesting happens, because that little child wants to see what it is. This curiosity, this desire to make some kind of sense out of things, goes right to the heart of the kind of creatures that we are.

Children are not only extremely good at learning; they are much better at it than we are. As a teacher, it took me a long time to find this out. I was an ingenious and resourceful teacher, clever about thinking up lesson plans and demonstrations and motivating devices and all of that acamaracus. And I only very slowly and painfully—believe me, painfully—learned that when I started teaching less, the children started learning more.

I can sum up in five to seven words what I eventually learned as a teacher. The seven-word version is: Learning is not the product of teaching. The five-word version is: Teaching does not make learning. As I mentioned before, organized education operates on the assumption that children learn only when and only what and only because we teach them. This is not true. It is very close to one hundred percent false.

Learners make learning. Learners create learning. The reason that this has been forgotten is that the activity of learning has been made into a product called "education," just as the activity, the discipline, of caring for one's health has become the product of "medical care," and the activity of inquiring into the world has become the product of "science," a specialized thing presumably done only by people with billions of dollars of complicated apparatus. But health is not a product and science is something you and I do every day of our lives. In fact, the word *science* is synonymous with the word *learning*.

What do we do when we make learning, when we create learning? Well, we observe, we look, we listen. We touch, taste, smell, manipulate, and sometimes measure or calculate. And then we wonder, we say, "Well, why this?" or "Why is it this way?" or "Did this thing make this thing happen?" or "What made this thing happen?" or "Can we make it happen differently or better?" or "Can we get the Mexican bean beetle off the beans?" or "Can we raise more fruit?" or "Can we fix the washing machine?" or whatever it might be. And then we invent theories, what scientists call hypotheses; we make hunches, we say, "Well, maybe it's because of this," or "Perhaps it's because of that," or "Maybe if I do this, this will happen." And then we test these theories or these hypotheses.

We may test them simply by asking questions of people we think know more than we do, or we may test them by further observation. We may say, "Well, I don't quite know what that thing is, but maybe if I watch it longer I will find out." Or maybe we do some kind of planned experiment—"Well, I'll try putting this on the beans and see if it does something to the bean beetles," or "I'll try doing something else." And from these, in various ways, we either find out that our hunch was not so good, or perhaps that it was fairly good, and then we go on, we observe some more, we speculate some more. We ask more questions, we make more theories, we test them.

This process creates learning, and we all do it. It's not just done by people at M.I.T. or Rensselaer Polytechnic. We do it. And this is exactly what children do. They are hard at work at this process all their waking hours. When they're not actually eating and sleeping, they're creating knowledge. They are observing, thinking, speculating, theorizing, testing, and experimenting—all the time—and they're much better at it than we are. The idea, the very idea, that we can teach small children how to learn has come to me to seem utterly absurd.

161

As I was writing this, there came, as if by wonderful coincidence, a long letter from a parent. At one point she says something that is so good that it could be a title for this book: "Every Time I Think of Something to Teach Them They Already Know It."

Children learn from anything and everything they see. They learn wherever they are, not just in special learning places. They learn much more from things, natural or made, that are real and significant in the world in their own right and not just made in order to help children learn; in other words, they are more interested in the objects and tools that we use in our regular lives than in almost any special learning materials made for them. We can best help children learn, not by deciding what we think they should learn and thinking of ingenious ways to teach it to them, but by making the world, as far as we can, accessible to them, paying serious attention to what they do, answering their questions— if they have any—and helping them explore the things they are most interested in. The ways we can do this are simple and easily understood by parents and other people who like children and will take the trouble to pay some attention to what they do and think about what it may mean. In short, what we need to know to help children learn is not obscure, technical, or complicated, and the materials we can use to help them lie ready at hand all around us.

A B O U T   T H E   A U T H O R

JOHN HOLT (1923–1985), writer, educator, lecturer, and amateur musician, wrote ten books, including *How Children Fail, How Children Learn, Never Too Late*, and *Teach Your Own*. His work has been translated into fourteen languages. *How Children Fail*, which the *New York Review of Books* rated as "in a class with Piaget," has sold over a million copies in its many editions. John Holt, for years a leading figure in school reform, became increasingly interested in how children learn outside school. The magazine he founded, *Growing without Schooling*, continues to reflect his philosophy. It is published by Holt Associates, 2269 Massachusetts Avenue, Cambridge, MA 02140.

Words in Color (Gattegno),
5
Writing, 12–43
  how not to learn, 31–35
  power of, 35
  as a process, 131–32
  and speaking, 16, 18, 31–
  34

Wyeth, Andrew, 11
Wyeth, N.C., 11

Yale School of Music, 109
Yellow Pages, 12

Zelan, Karen, 28–30

Flexischooling

Education for tomorrow, starting yesterday

by **Roland Meighan**

Dr. Roland Meighan, a Senior Lecturer in Education at Birmingham University, points out that ;

"...the complexities of modern life are such that, without the experience of behaving with considerable flexibility, people are at risk."

An effective education must prepare people for this modern world. It follows that it should, itself, employ flexible and varied approaches.

For many years, Roland Meighan has been one of the few researchers into education who has taken seriously the motivation, practice and views of parents who have wished to educate their children "otherwise" than at school. At the same time, he has, for 12 years, been training teachers for the real business of educating by teaching in a way that enables learning. He has taught students in a democratic way so as to involve them fundamentally in their own learning about teaching. Now he applies the whole of this experience to a blueprint for the regeneration of education - an education flexible enough to serve the needs of the individuals living in our post-industrial society in the throes of a technological and communications revolution.

In "FLEXISCHOOLING", Roland Meighan demonstrates that there is a wide range of variations to consider in each of the main components of education - the Parents, the Learners, the Teachers, Locations where learning can take place, the Curriculum, the Resources for learning - and opens up possibilities far beyond the conventional, narrow forms we are used to.

Flexischooling: more than a dream

"...some teachers have tried, usually against heavy odds, to develop more flexible approaches. Braving hostile and hysterical journalists, the unimaginative reactions of H.M.I's (themselves victims of the system), and incredulous colleagues, they have sought to break out of the existing rigidities. ...examples can be found of more flexible educational practice, not from the home-school movement, but from within the schools. Indeed, the answer to those who say that flexischooling could never happen is that substantial elements of it are already here."

THE AUTHOR

Dr Roland Meighan is a Senior Lecturer in Education at the University of Birmingham and has also been associated with the Open University since its inception. He has worked in primary, secondary and further education in the U.K. and he has also had experience of the Local Authority Inspectorate. He is an editor of *Educational Review* and the author or co-author of over fifty publications including *Schools, Pupils and Deviance; Perspectives on Society; Schooling, Ideology and the Curriculum; Alternative Educational Futures; A Sociology of Educating* and *The Democratic School*. His research work includes a ten year study of the perspectives of pupils and their judgements of teaching, an ongoing study now in its twelfth year of parents who opt to educate their children at home, and action research into democratic learning co-operatives as a method of teacher training.

ISBN 1 871526 00 0

£5.95

Obtainable from Education Now, P.O.Box 186, Ticknall, Derbyshire DE7 1WF.